PRESCRIPTIVE TEACHING

PRESCRIPTIVE TEACHING

THEORY INTO PRACTICE

By

Norma Banas, M.Ed.

Curriculum Director
Educational Guidance Services, Inc.
Miami, Florida

I.H.Wills, M.S.

Diagnostic Director
Educational Guidance Services, Inc.
Miami, Florida

With Illustrations by
SHARON S. HENDERSON

CHARLES C THOMAS • PUBLISHER
Springfield • Illinois • U.S.A.

Published and Distributed Throughout the World by
CHARLES C THOMAS • PUBLISHER
Bannerstone House
301-327 East Lawrence Avenue, Springfield, Illinois, U.S.A.

© *1977, by* CHARLES C THOMAS • PUBLISHER

ISBN 0-398-03546-6
Library of Congress Catalog Card Number: 76-4963

*With THOMAS BOOKS careful attention is given to all details of
manufacturing and design. It is the Publisher's desire to present books that are
satisfactory as to their physical qualities and artistic possibilities and
appropriate for their particular use. THOMAS BOOKS will be true to those
laws of quality that assure a good name and good will.*

Printed in the United States of America
R-11

Library of Congress Cataloging in Publication Data

Banas, Norma.
    Prescriptive teaching.

    Bibliography: p.
    Includes index.
    1. Perceptual-motor learning. 2. Slow learning
children. I. Wills, I. H., joint author. II. Title.
LB1067.B27   371.9'043   76-4963
ISBN 0-398-03546-6

INTRODUCTION

T HIS BOOK was prepared for use in methods courses at the college level for teachers in elementary education, special education, secondary education, and clinical reading departments. It can also be of value as a basic text on learning needs for psychologists, guidance counselors, school administrators, and others who will be working with student's adjustment problems related to school success.

Prescriptive Teaching: Theory into Practice is the outgrowth of fifteen years of work by the authors in the field of specific learning disabilities. It is written with the hope that their experiences can be of help to *all* students in developing skills for successful learning.

According to one recent survey by the Department of Health, Education, and Welfare, there are ten million children in the United States with "learning disabilities." By this is meant children of average or above average intellectual potential who are not functioning to their potential because of an interference in one or more of the learning pathways. This interference is not due to physical handicaps, visual, speech, or motor dysfunction, mental retardation, primary emotional disturbance, or environmental disadvantage.

In every classroom there are students who have been diagnosed or suspected as having a learning disability who will benefit immeasurably from the approaches in this text. But more importantly, there are also students in these same classrooms who may not be learning at their optimum levels, but who would show improved learning rates and greater depth of understanding of what they learn through these same approaches.

This book is intended to provide theory and insight into the development of the skills needed for successful learning experiences. Theory, methods, and materials are provided and fully illustrated in the areas of visual, visual/motor, auditory, and language function, perception, and memory as they relate to learning. These methods were originally developed in a clinical situation, but they have been successfully adapted for use in small groups and tried in regular classrooms.

It is a generally accepted fact that each individual learns more effectively through one pathway than another. The pattern of strengths and weaknesses provides us with a profile or picture of a person's "learning mode." In two previous publications the authors set down guidelines for the assessment of the students' strengths and weaknesses.

Learning is a developmental process, and it is important to be sure a basic skill is present before moving on to the next level skill. Therefore, the text is

v

carefully structured in a step-by-step developmental manner. Each section provides therapeutic approaches to hasten development of identified lags or weaknesses in the learning mode. Each section provides training at the three-dimensional level and proceeds in a systematic manner to the abstract or linear level, being careful to provide activities which will insure transfer of learning from the concrete to the linear level.

The words *error-free reinforcement* are used over and over again in this text. The authors cannot emphasize too frequently that trial-and-error exercises or activities are an ineffective means of learning for the perceptually handicapped child. Initial intake must be accurate for recall to be accurate. Thus, the development of key cards as static visual clues becomes an integral part of the methods presented.

Tutoring is an ineffective means of helping a child with a basic lag or deficiency in his learning mode, as it acts, at best, as a Band-Aid® over the problem. The design and nature of this text will help educators provide a program to develop more effective learning skills.

A fully clinical one-to-one or small group program can be designed from this text for the remediation of learning deficits or for the improvement of learning efficiency in general. The classroom teacher can use the special teaching techniques and materials and individualized home assignments designed to teach the students to compensate by working through their strengths.

With this dual purpose, this text hopefully will provide for students both a program to strengthen developmental lags and one to help them work through their open pathways while therapy is being provided.

ACKNOWLEDGMENTS

THE BEGINNINGS of this book are rooted in the start given to us at the University of Miami Reading Clinic where Dr. L. R. Wheeler taught us the need for consistency; Dr. Ed Smith encouraged our interest in research, and Dr. Emmett Betts gave us a foundation from which to work.

This textbook has been over ten years in the growing process, which began when Mrs. Frances McGlannan exposed us to the need for the associative learning method and encouraged experimentation and hard work in developing new approaches to working with children with learning problems. During our five years at the McGlannan School many of these methods were initiated. Since founding Educational Guidance Services, Inc. in 1967, these methods have been modified, clarified, and new directions have led to new approaches.

Many professionals expressed confidence in our work and encouraged our continued growth. We wish to give special thanks to Dr. DeForest Strunk, who gave us a feeling for the exceptional child and encouraged us to share our work with others; to Dr. Robert Allen, who shares his diagnostic knowledge and encourages, never discourages, constant investigation; Dr. Jack Benson, who has helped us integrate information from the field of audiology and speech; to Drs. Agnes Austin and Robert Tanner, who helped show us the importance of vision in learning; and to Dr. Jack Liberman for whom vision is a way of life. A special thank-you goes to Dr. Betty Rowen, who has shared with us her vast knowledge and love of early childhood development, which led us into extending our work to preventive therapy at the preschool level.

Our greatest debt of thanks goes to our staff, who have helped to make this book a reality. Mrs. Sandra Felton contributed her creative genius in trying and refining methods of teaching math and English grammar to severely perceptually impaired students. Mrs. Eleonor Van Wagner used her training in speech and language development in teaching listening for reading and spelling. Mrs. Frances Sachs has used her awareness of the need for data and organization to teach upper-level students how to extract, organize, and hold subject matter.

Words are not enough to express our indebtedness to our administrative assistant and friend, Mrs. Ann Murray, who has for many years forced us to crystallize our ideas by her astute questions, and whose work on this manuscript has been tireless.

To Mrs. Jane McLeod goes our thanks for keeping all the little pieces from getting lost and for helping make many of the methods come to life in practice with our preschoolers, with whom her work is invaluable. Mrs. Beverly Yelen, our diagnostic assistant, uses her training to identify problems as she works with students, and stimulates new directions for us as she continues to prod us with the yet-to-be-solved problems.

And thanks to Don Cundy, who helped to point out the need each student has, no matter how young, for self-awareness of his own strengths and problems, so that goals can be realistic, and the fear of the unknown is removed.

Last, but by no means least, out thanks go to the wonderful, exciting, frustrating, rewarding children who have gone through our clinic or with whom we have come in contact, who have made these methods a reality.

N.B.
I.H.W.

CONTENTS

PRESCRIPTIVE TEACHING

Chapter 1

When b becomes d becomes p . . .

Position in space

BODY AWARENESS

THE ACCURATE perception of objects in relation to each other begins with perception of their relationship to oneself and stems from accurate perception and knowledge of one's own body.

Body image is a person's subjective experience of his own body – his feeling of it. It includes the awareness and the impression a person has of himself and can be observed in drawings of a person made by the student, as well as by his attitude and responses about himself.

Body concept is the intellectual knowledge of his body. It is acquired by conscious learning of the parts of his body and their functions and is reflected when he accurately attaches word labels and knows how his body is organized.

Body awareness is an automatic, unconscious ability to move through space, gained from the child's experiences as he moves his body through space. Smooth movements, good balance, and spatial concepts depend upon good body awareness.

A child's ability to coordinate eye and hand and to correctly perceive both his position in space and the relationship of symbols to himself and to each other depends upon the development of adequate body awareness.

The perceptually impaired child can be likened to the child who is blind or partially sighted. Blind children can develop good body image and spatial awareness (Cratty, 1971). This is done through movement education, as should be all spatial development for the learning disability child.

POSITION IN SPACE

Perception of position in space may be defined as perception of the relationship of an object to the observer. Spatially, at least, a person is

Portions of the material in this book are reprinted in a modified form from the authors' book, *Success Begins with Understanding,* 1972, with permission from Academic Therapy Publications of San Rafael, California.

always the center of his own world and perceives objects as being behind, before, above, below, or to the side of himself.

In order that the relationship of the body to other objects be developed, the child moves through his world physically. As he climbs through barrels, climbs over obstacles, goes under, around, and in objects, he begins to know where his body is in relation to these objects and how much space his body uses up. Later he will learn to make judgments from vision alone, but not until he has had sufficient kinesthetic experience.

A classroom or physical education area can be converted into an obstacle course aimed at giving experiences in all types of relationships of body to object(s) outside the body.* A multitude of experiences can be converted into useful learning experiences. The possibilities are almost endless. Two criteria are important, however. (1) Activity must in some way enrich the child's awareness of his own body. This must include eyes-closed experiences which require internal awareness of the body. (2) Activity should include verbalizing at all times to add a simultaneous auditory/kinesthetic match and bring in another learning avenue, as well as to develop accurate language.

---

*An excellent program is outlined in N. C. Kephart's *Slow Learner in the Classroom,* Columbus, Merrill, 1971.

Ask the children to lie on a flat surface. Call off various body parts and have the children touch that part while they say the name. Have them work *with eyes closed.* Repeat this exercise in different body positions. Do not allow the children to look at the part to be touched.

Throw a beach ball at a child, calling off a body part, to which he must respond by hitting the ball back with that part.

Play follow the leader. Have children *say each action* as they do it. Verbal instructions should be given singly or in sequence. Example: "Go under the desk, then around the box."

Hold up a picture of a person and an object (may be in a box, on the desk, etc.). Have one child execute the action shown in the picture. Team competition may create further interest.

One child may execute an action in relation to an object or objects. Another child must then imitate accurately this action or sequence.

Have a child stand in front of a chalkboard (then at his desk on paper which is placed on a slant board) and draw lines as directed, "Up," "down," etc., in relation to his body. Have him verbalize the action.

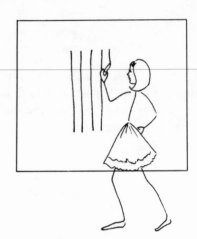

Each pupil has an object and follows the teacher's directions to "move the (car) toward you, move the (car) up," etc., always saying the action involved.

BODY CONCEPT: A STEP-BY-STEP UNDERSTANDING

Exercises in body awareness are closely related to directionality and to position in space: specifically they are needed in reading and writing.

By examining his own body the child can learn about the joints, about the lengths, widths, and directions of his limbs and their relationship to his body.

These experiences with his body can then be translated into clay, pipe cleaner people, or puppet people.

A simple plastic doll with jointed arms, legs, and head should be used as a model when building the clay people.

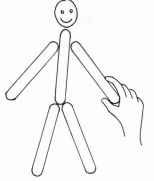

Popsicle® stick people can provide knowledge of a moving figure, its relationship to objects, and its relationship to other persons.

These stick figures may then be pasted onto art paper and a background drawn around them or they may be stood in a doll house or play setting.

Cardboard figures in profile, put together limb by limb and joined with paper fasteners, can be moved at the joints to learn movement patterns.*

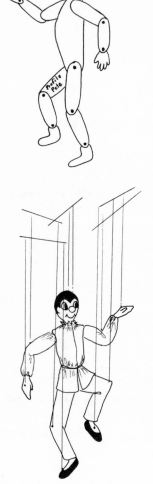

Puppets offer experiences in body movement, and plays can be used effectively in extended activities of a variety of natures.

Ask the child to pretend that he is a puppet and that he has imaginary strings attached to his limbs. Verbally tell him the string that you are pulling and have him move that limb in puppet fashion. If this is too difficult or if the child has an auditory perception problem, show him a puppet and demonstrate how it works. Then, actually attach the string to his arms and legs and gently pull on the string to identify which part of the body he should move. When this is learned, remove the strings and point to the limb to be moved.

*Profile Pete, Open Court Kindergarten Program, LaSalle, Illinois.

Using a drum, beat out a simple rhythm. Have the group walk in a circle in time with the beat (fast, slow, etc.). Suggest they feel large (tall), small, etc., and show this in their movements.

Have children imitate the movement (and antics) of animals. "How does a monkey walk?" Help them feel the part by telling a story or use story records as they improvise movement.

Have child or children imitate playing an active game. Let the class guess what they are doing (batting a ball, bowling).

Have a child dance around in a circle using all varieties of body movements. When teacher claps his hands, the child should "freeze" in whatever position he is at that moment. Other children copy the pose.

Hold up a large, clear picture of a person in a specific pose. Have the class adopt the pose in the picture. Demonstrate, if necessary.

Hold up a large, clear picture of a person in a particular pose. Have the class position their cardboard person in the same position.

Have the children draw a stick picture to imitate movement seen. They should begin with concrete images and develop through the abstract. Let them learn from themselves, others, pictures, and symbols.

BODY CONCEPT REINFORCED VISUALLY

Once familiarity is obtained with the body, more abstract visual activities may replace the initial concrete kinesthetic involvement. Do not move to this step too quickly, as a child may have more difficulty translating the visual impression than the kinesthetic impression. Remembering that the body is the point of origin for all movements and for all interpretations of outside relationships, the teacher should provide enough reinforcement and review in as varied a setting as possible. Always have the child name the parts as he works, so that he develops language as well.

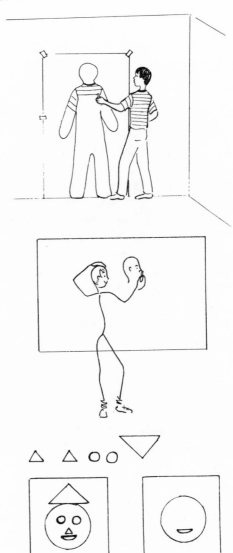

Have the student stand against a full person-sized sheet of paper taped to the wall. Draw around his form. Now have him investigate his body and fill in the proper position of his clothing and facial features.

Have the child draw himself on the chalkboard, one feature at a time by checking his own body.

Fill in missing parts of a face or incomplete person on a mimeographed sheet.

Provide different colored squares, triangles, circles, and other shapes cut from construction paper. Have the child copy a model built by the teacher.

If the position of the pieces in relation to each other proves to be a problem, the model and the child's paper may be ruled with guidelines; or, the paper may be dittoed with the outline of the pieces and the pieces inserted into the matching places.

Find large, simple pictures of faces and of people. Make a copy of each. Paste one of each picture onto cardboard and cut them into even puzzle strips. Keep one picture whole as a model. Have the child build the puzzle by matching while he names the body parts as he works. This helps focus his attention on meaningful matching. Do not allow him to match color or insignificant details. Be sure he works by matching body parts.

A. J. Kirshner has an excellent program called Kirshner Body Alphabet, which not only adds to body awareness but utilizes this basic learning level as the child internalizes the forms of the alphabet.

BODY AWARENESS AND DIFFERENTIATING LEFT AND RIGHT

The ability to properly attach the words *left* and *right* does not indicate good body awareness. However, these terms will be important to school success and should be taught at the body awareness level, rather than as a language lesson.

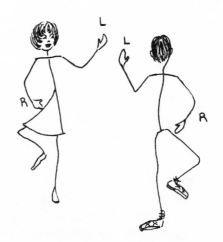

Have the child face the teacher (or other child) and copy positions using the same side (right to right).

Have the child face a mirror and copy the teacher's positions. To insure positive practice when using the words *left* and *right* be sure to have a meaningful clue for the child to refer to such as placing an *L* or an *R* as a clue on each hand and foot.

Have the child face a mirror and execute positions called to him.

Simon Says can be used to develop body concepts, left-right differentiation, and perception of position in space. Tell the group to stamp the right foot, raise the left hand, etc. Eliminate each as he fails until a winner remains. Before beginning, put an *L* and an *R* as a clue on each hand and foot.

Show pictures of parts of the body asking for each, "Is it the left.., or the right...?" If the child cannot answer correctly, have him compare his own body part to the picture image. Continue to label the child's body to indicate left and right. Do not label the pictures.

Show pictures of a person putting on clothing. Have one of a pair missing and ask, "Which . . . is missing?" or "Which foot has the shoe on?" etc.

which shoe is off?

Show pictures of a person or persons and ask the child to identify his right or left arm, leg, etc. Develop this ability using positions facing the child, going in the same direction, and sideways.

BODY AWARENESS AND NUMBER READINESS

According to Piaget's concepts of cognitive development (Ginsburg and Opper, 1969), number concepts are dependent on the level of awareness the child has obtained of his environment. The child from two to seven has not yet recognized rules and concepts outside his own physical world. He has not yet learned cause and effect, so that relationship of events or objects may not be correct. Between the years of seven to eleven the child becomes increasingly less involved with himself and begins to think of more than one thing at a time; he can think in terms of the whole and its parts simultaneously, and he can learn that one thing follows another in series. He is aware of himself as something apart from the total environment and begins to see that the rules which relate to that environment are not changing as he is, but are constant and repetitive.

As he develops this sense of awareness of himself as separate from the total environment, he recognizes spatial relationships and begins to develop number concepts. Piaget described the approach to this stage by providing the child with two containers which hold the same amount, with one tall and narrow, and the other short and broad. The child who cannot conceive of them having the same volume is not ready for number concepts.

By translating space into body awareness, the child should be able to visualize and understand that the same volume of space is required when he sits as when he stands. All the obstacle course exercises would contribute to development of this concept, as the concepts of size and space are recognized as he moves his body through space.

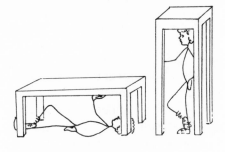

The concept that one and one make two requires being able to think simultaneously of the whole and its parts and to make associations between the parts and the whole. Body concept and the fact that the body is made up of corresponding and symmetrical parts leads to an awareness of association.

Our ten fingers and toes are the basis of the tens number system and should be used in developing numbers as units of larger and smaller amounts. Do not let a child count from one in identifying, "How many fingers do I have up?" To insure transfer from the concrete (body) level to the abstract (symbol) level, have the students write the number represented by the raised fingers. Alternate this with showing a number card and have the students show with their fingers what amount that symbol represents. It is essential that the experience and its symbol referent be presented together.

It is also important in the development of number value to learn the "feel" of quantities. Provide a divider board with a hole cut in the bottom, through which the child can place his hand. Place groups of buttons, beans, or similar objects on one side. Have the student learn to recognize the amount *without counting.* This should be presented first as, "Feel this amount; it is one bean (or two or three, etc. to ten)." Next, "What is this amount you feel?" Reinforce the correct answer if he falters. Teach him the "feel" of one through ten items in random placement. Have him write the number he feels.

Measurement concepts should be developed first using the body as an indicator of distance (without actual measurements). "If you extended your arm across the table, where would it reach?" How many paces would it take to reach the doorway? How many hand widths is the table?" etc.

The symbol referents for volumes can be developed while experiencing the concept of volume, as when pouring from one size container to another if the containers used are always labeled. Thus, the relationships of one measure to another are developed as the concept of space is being experienced.

The child must also be able to reverse his thinking, if he is to be able to handle processes such as subtraction. To develop this process, he must be able to experience adding to and taking away from the total. The body awareness training should be given in front of a mirror, or with a partner, emphasizing recognition and reproduction of the visual image in reverse. The use of fingers can be continued in adding to and taking away from.

Then fingers are used again, but this time in adding and subtracting fashion. "Show me . . . , now show me . . . put them together and what do we have?" Have students see the symbols problem they are doing with their fingers. Reverse and hold up your fingers, "How many fingers do I have up? How many more do I have up? How many in all do I now have?" Students write the problem and answer as viewed.

Repeat this process with the child feeling through the divider board of beans or buttons. Touch the child's hand to one pile, "How many buttons do you feel? Move his hand to another pile. "How many buttons do you feel? Combine the piles, and how many buttons do you have?"

POSITION IN SPACE AND TIME AWARENESS

The child uses space awareness in interpreting his environment, but he also uses a time awareness. This is developed as he moves through space by an awareness of how long it takes to cover distances or how much time is consumed between his own movements in executing a task. Tapping a finger fast or slow is a time awareness. The need for a coordination of the body in sequencing its movements or its rhythms is essential to allow one to develop the space/time concept. In order to measure or sense the concept of time, movement in space must be repetitive. When there is interference in the rhythms, there is difficulty organizing space/time.

Adequate control and awareness of time structure depends on the development and use of the body's natural rhythms.

Hop and Skip

Hopping and skipping require balance, laterality, and rhythm. They require the child to shift the weight from one side of his body to another, while he keeps an alternating pattern of sequential movement and a smooth rhythm.

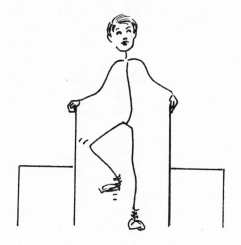

Place two small chairs (seat facing out) approximately two and one-half feet apart. The child stands in between chairs, placing right hand on top of right chair, left hand on top of left chair. First, he lifts one foot off the ground, holding on to the chair, then the other foot. If the child is not able to lift one foot at a time and hold it up for three seconds, the teacher may actually lift the child's foot.

The child alternates right and left, lifting his feet; this is done to a rhythmic, slow beat (teacher calls out or claps hands). Colored tape (red for right, green for left) may be placed on each shoe for a reminder of the terms *left/right.* As confidence is gained, one chair is removed. The child then hops with his left, then his right foot, holding on only with one hand.

The second chair is now removed, but placed close by in case the child needs to grab hold. He proceeds to hop, alternating slowly, then picks up speed and moves forward slightly when the raised foot returns to the ground. This alternating forward hop is the skipping movement.

Jumping

A springboard is used as the first step in learning to jump. The student stands on the board without shoes.

The child stands in the middle of the board; if he is fearful the teacher holds his hands. He bounces up and down to a steady rhythmic beat, while looking out at eye level at a fixed spot. Jump activities should be done to nursery rhymes or chants for aid and stress on rhythm.

With his confidence building, the child now repeats the rhythmic bounce without the teacher's assistance.

The teacher stands next to the springboard and holds his hand six inches above the student's head. The student tries to touch the teacher's hand as he bounces each time. (Do not let the child look up.)

Have the student, with his eyes closed, try to remain in one spot when jumping up and down.

Next, introduce jumping on and jumping off the board. If needed, the teacher may assist by holding the child's hand at first. Proceed to eyes-closed jumping on and off.

A Hoola Hoop® is now provided for each child. After the child has enjoyed playing with the hoop in experimentation and play, it is introduced as a second prejump step.

The hoop is held by the teacher in both hands, hooped over the child's head, then lowered down his body (without touching the body) until it reaches his feet. The child is then to jump forward through the hoop using both feet at the same time. Teach him to anticipate the downward movement and to be ready to jump over the descended hoop as it arrives at ground level. A slow beat should be used to increase synchronization.

Introduce the jump rope at this point. It is better for the teacher to tie one end of the rope to a door knob or hook than to try to turn a rope in conjunction with another student. An inexperienced rope turner may cause additional problems for the child just developing rhythm and synchronized movements. Verbalizing by the rope turner and the jumper is a must as an aid to rhythm.

The student at first is instructed to jump over the rope (with both feet) while it is lying on the ground. The rope is then raised six to eight inches and he again practices jumping over the still slack rope.

The teacher now introduces the game, High Water, Low Water. (This game is less a jump activity and more a method to develop body awareness in space). The rope is poised above the student's head, and he runs through or under it as it is lowered behind him, making appropriate forward adjustments so that the rope doesn't touch his back as it is allowed to fall to the ground behind him.

The child is now ready to work with the moving rope. He stands on the spot on the floor marked with an *X*. For a few tries, the rope is just swung along the floor *slowly*, while the student jumps with both feet together over the moving rope. He is to try to remain on the *X* at all times.

The child is now told not to jump until the teacher's command, "Jump." The rope is fully rotated, and the teacher counts, "one, two, three . . ." When the rope is nearly

at the child's ankle, the teacher commands, "Jump." Thus the child can concern himself with only lifting his feet off the ground at the appropriate moment. This method is continued until the child feels the rhythm and can jump a few times in a row.

After a while, the teacher only gives the "jump" command at the first turn of the rope and the child does the rest. Nursery rhymes or chants are called by the child and waiting classmates to keep the steady, flowing rhythm.

The child can be taught via teacher demonstration and practice on the springboard (using no rope) the "middle bounce." After a few successful practices, he attempts to jump rope with this added bounce.

As proficiency increases, variations may be introduced: i.e. eyes-closed jumping, very good for building awareness of body spatial relations.

The child is now ready to attempt jump rope on an individual basis. His feet know what to do, but he has to learn to coordinate his arm movements with his jump.

He must be shown how to use his arms in moving them in a slow circle from the back of his ankle, outward and upward to over his head, and downward again. When he takes the rope in his hand and executes the proper movements, he

must jump at the same moment the rope reaches the floor in front of his ankles. Have him practice with a hoola hoop at first, then a rope.

At first, the teacher should again command, "Jump," so the student is free to concentrate on his arm movements. The nursery rhyme or chant is provided and the child learns to say the rhyme as he jumps.

TIME: A SPATIAL/TEMPORAL AWARENESS

Time is a spatial/temporal awareness. It is a feeling of the amount of time one takes to get from one place to another. This is projected into past and future time as lapses since being in a place or until going to another place. The first time referents were verbalized as, "I will meet you in the length of time it takes to milk the cow," as this was a commonly shared (though far from exact) experience of comparable measure. To record specific (time) spans now we have affixed words and developed a symbol system.

However, the first or basic clock is the internal clock which is felt to be related to basic body rhythms. If one could not repeat an action in the same way (rhythmically), he would not be able to develop a consistent feel for a span of time.

Some children do not seem to have developed a time sense and constantly ask, "Is it a minute? Is it tomorrow?" etc. The following activities can be used to help these children develop a better time sense.

Teach the students to tap their feet, fingers, or nod their heads to the beat of a metronome. A metronome provides both a visual and an auditory clue to help follow its rhythm.

Set a timer for short, but specific, periods of time (one minute, twice that much, etc.). Have the children tap their feet, fingers, etc., or walk around the room and *feel* how long it takes to use up that time span (signalled when the timer rings). After many repeater experiences of the same span, ask them to try to guess when to stop and to stop just before the timer goes off. See how closely they can guess.

Relate time span to activities that the children are accustomed to. "Tomorrow is when you awaken in the morning, a full day is from breakfast today to breakfast tomorrow, five days are the days you go to school, two days are the days you are not in school, twenty minutes is our school lunch time, etc." Now, measure unknown time spans against a known time span. "How long will it take us to do our arithmetic?" Measure the time span by how much of the class period (of known time) the arithmetic took. "We still can do about four more activities, so it took us one-fourth of an hour period, or it took us about fifteen minutes."

Chapter 2

Spatial relations

S PATIAL relations is defined as involving the ability of an observer to perceive the position of two or more objects in relation to himself and in relation to each other.

All of our information regarding spatial locations comes to us through movement experience. Through the translation of movement into space we obtain knowledge of the distance of an object from ourselves. "Space" then becomes essentially a concept perceived by the brain and later translated automatically by the eyes.

The importance of spatial awareness is also observed in working with numbers or arithmetic. Stabilizing the spatial world is the most complicated of our readiness skills and develops last in the series of visual perceptual skills.

An imperfect sense of rhythm can cause problems in reciting in correct sequence such data as days of the week and causes confusion of time incidents and of important occasions in history.

It should be noted that children develop abilities in space perception in an ordered fashion. First, they develop understanding of topological space as represented in such concepts as nearness, separation, enclosure, and continuation. Then, they begin to perceive and understand projective space involving figures in relation to each other in coordinate systems, perspective, and various geometric measures.

The young child learns to recognize objects from all angles; so the preschool child reverses letters until taught that, although a cup is a cup in any position,

letters have a fixed position for identification, *b,d,p,g;* yet, even letter forms can vary and remain the same symbol.

$$a \quad a \quad a$$

Children need to be consciously introduced to the concept of sameness as being synonymous with position, rather than for likeness of form. At the same time they must be consciously taught to work and view from left to right.

Motor control, eye/motor coordination, and spatial awareness, if poor, can affect playing ball games (catching a ball in flight), learning to ride a bicycle, and constructing jigsaw puzzles, drawing, copying, and writing, among other things.

PART-TO-WHOLE PERCEPTION

Horizontal spatial relations can be developed with sequential picture designs. Always develop the picture sequence from left to right. Provide ditto sheets similar to that illustrated — a blank sheet and a variety of colored paper shapes. Models should progress from a colored, raised pattern to a colored, linear (lines drawn on paper) pattern to a linear outline.

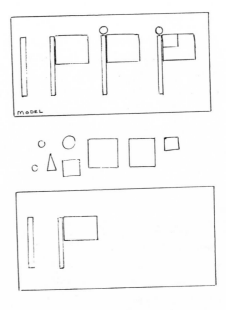

Copying and construction of this sequence is done kinesthetically with precut forms from which to choose and place on a construction sheet as the model illustrates. Work *must* be from left to right only.

Next a pattern sequence may be copied with a pencil directly on the paper.

Geometric shapes cut from construction paper can be used by the child to copy simple patterns; this develops an ability needed in seeing part to whole.

Begin with a simple single figure pattern, such as a flower or a person.

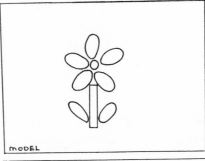

Proceed to multiform scenes. Later, allow the child freedom to create his own pictures. Working with cut-out construction paper shapes in this way helps bridge the gap between the three-dimensional environment and the two-dimensional and linear environment.

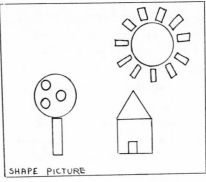

Provide commercially available games or books where the activity requires that the child punch out pictures to be matched and inserted into a scene in order to complete that scene. Visual matching is the basic skill required. Color and context clues help accurate matching.

CUT OUT THE PIECES BELOW AND ASSEMBLE AT THE RIGHT

Assemble body parts by cutting and pasting onto a model, as with a puzzle, to create an understanding of part-to-whole development. Body concept and spatial clues should be provided. Exercises like this one are included in Frostig and Horne's *Frostig Program for the Development of Visual Perception.*

Tiles in the shape of triangles, squares, and rectangles (commercially available) and pegboards should be used with a model made to actual size and color. Have the child match by placing his piece on the model for the correct spatial position, then placing the piece on his board. When working to a model, the model must be placed at the left side of the work space to insure left-to-right viewing and work habits.

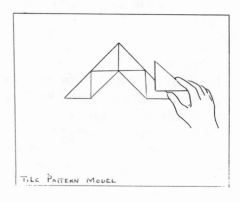

TILE PATTERN MODEL

Make tile designs which represent letters of the alphabet. Later the child can work from models which are smaller (representative) of the finished picture he will make.

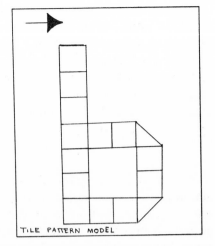

TILE PATTERN MODEL

Commercially available sets of play tiles provide complex pictures to be reproduced on the tile board. This requires an advanced skill to follow previous reproduction of designs only.

Next, provide duplicator models in linear form from which the child must copy the design by shape and position alone. (At all steps, the child is using the kinesthetic approach of building with tiles, rather than reproduction with paper and pencil.) He must also verbalize as he works.

Dot books employing numbers in sequence or alphabet in sequence are invaluable in helping establish eye/hand control and part-to-whole awareness. Each child, until proficient with the alphabet or his numbers, should have a key card with the correct sequence from which he may guide himself in his book. Ask him to connect the dots until he can guess what is on the picture, and then continue and see if he is correct.

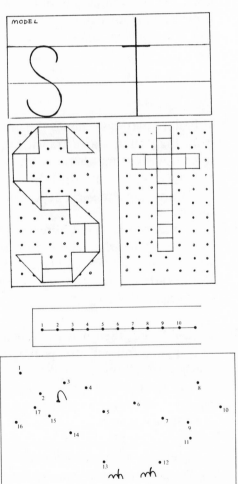

Pegboards can be used with golf tees. The child copies a pattern first from a comparable board, *then* from a duplicator sheet. If he cannot recognize the pattern, he may need to have the model and his board numbered by rows and columns to act as a guide to position in space.

Patterns must be developed from simple, single lines varied in length and placement, and in various horizontal, vertical, and diagonal positions. Then complex double and triple patterns of parallel, adjacent, and interlocking lines are to be used.

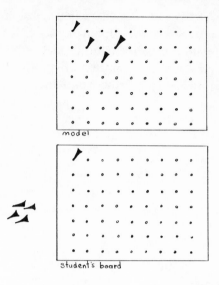

Letter patterns should emerge from this training as a transitional stage from the kinesthetic eye/hand activity to the visual (using the eyes to identify size and space) eye/hand activity.

In this work many directional errors begin to arise. The use of an arrow to remind the child to start at the left and the top and move left to right *is essential.*

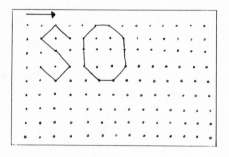

Chalkboard, then paper and pencil copying follows the pegboard experiences. Kephart (1971) outlines in detail procedures for training and patterns for development of copying at this stage.

Commercially available coloring books give guidance in another form of matching. Here, eye/hand activity, as well as matching, is required. Be sure that the child understands the color key system. Provide a copy of the key on a 3" x 5" file card, so that he can place it at the top of each page, as opposed to working from memory or by reference back to the initial page key.

Commercially available kits give the child experience in spatial relations through the placement of figures (some built from parts) on a background. There is also training in finger dexterity and size matching in this activity.

Jigsaw puzzles designed from large, simple pictures of a single object such as a person, an automobile, or an animal, give further experience in part-to-whole development. The child must match to a model and use spatial concepts (for example, the wheel goes below the running board). Children enjoy finding pictures and cutting them into puzzles for use by other classmates. They must never work by clues of color or shape of pieces, but by perceiving a missing segment of the picture.

Maps may also be traced, pasted on cardboard, then cut apart (by geographic units) into jigsaw puzzles. Have another outline map to which the puzzle is matched to develop accurate visual matching and error-free learning.

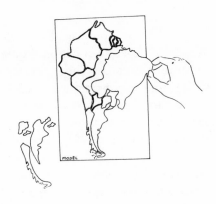

Mazes can be found in many children's books or made by the teacher. A sense of visual awareness of direction and planning ahead is necessary to complete mazes without being caught in the various traps and blockades. Choose mazes with well-defined walls. Progress from visually vivid paths to lesser clues until the child can accomplish a maze with pathways only. Always work with mazes from left to right.

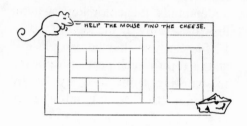

Floor plans are conceived as orientation in space. Begin by having the child copy from his immediate environment such as the classroom or his bedroom in a single room setting. Develop an ability to draw floor plans of a multiroom complex, then of unfamiliar settings described verbally.

Exercise books entitled "Map Readiness" are published by My Weekly Reader, Education Center, Columbus, Ohio. These booklets give training and practice in spatial orientation and directional relationships, but they need to be changed so that a kinesthetic experience can replace the visual-only instruction. General principles of kinesthetic involvement should be applied to work in these booklets.

LEFT/RIGHT SEQUENTIAL DEVELOPMENT

Geometric Shapes have been used by readiness programs to sort for discrimination of shape, color, size, and texture. However, the importance of the sequencing and the part-to-whole relationship of a word (which, when misconceived by a child, causes his reading, spelling, and writing disabilities) is often overlooked.

Use geometric shapes of cardboard or wood in a variety of shapes, sizes, and colors, or use geometric templates. Use blocks identical in shape and size but varied in color. Begin with a sequence of three, set up a pattern and have the child copy your pattern with his shapes. *Always work left to right.*

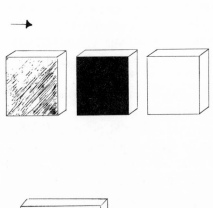

Add size variation, as well as color. Develop immediate or visual/motor memory by having the child build the pattern from copy, then remove the model and rebuild it from memory. Do this at each of the following steps. Have the child verbalize (aloud) the sequence as he views the model. This is a major boost to visual memory.

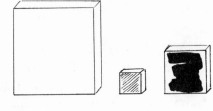

Add changes of shape as well as size and color. Continue as above.

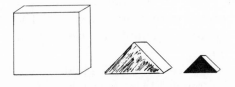

Reduce the intensity of the stimuli by using construction paper geometric shapes of a variety of shapes and sizes, but only black and white colors. Repeat the same step-by-step progression from simple to complex for direct copying and recall.

Eliminate the color clue. Make all black shapes, but vary size and shape. Proceed as above.

Provide linear sequence patterns drawn on duplicator sheets. Have the child reproduce the design, first using paper cut-out shapes, then drawing the shapes below the model pattern. Be sure to include a memory step as above.

Blocks of various colors (such as are available from Developmental Learning Materials, Niles, Illinois) can be used at this stage to combine sequencing as well as spatial arrangement and size relationships.

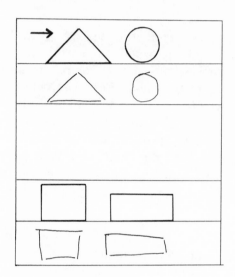

Provide a model (lined) work sheet and blocks. The teacher builds a pattern with her blocks as illustrated, which includes skipping of spaces as well as various lengths and placements. Only one base line is utilized to simulate the later formation of words on a line. The children reproduce with their blocks.

The teacher builds a pattern, but the pupils do not watch as it is built. They then reproduce it.

Later, patterns are built and reproduced with blocks on sheets having no guidelines.

Finally the model in picture form is copied with crayons as a linear-to-linear activity (first on lined, then on unlined paper).

Build one like my pattern.

The teacher presents a picture representing the block pattern. The children place their blocks on the model and then properly place it on their sheet.

SPATIAL RELATIONS APPLIED

Once oriented in spatial relations, the child must apply this skill to the development of words, sentences and stories.

Cartoon sequences viewed and recalled give visual emphasis to left/right progression in comprehension development. Story sequences completed after listening to the teacher tell a story lend reinforcement to mentally holding images in sequence.

Tracing, cutting out, and pasting of letters to form words, then matching to a model gives sequential spatial reinforcement in word building.

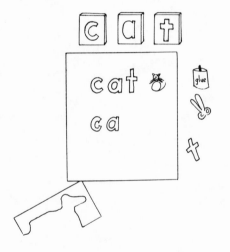

Working with coded messages gives the child motivating experiences with symbol placement in sequence. Attention must be paid to the parts as they form the total, for with coded symbols the child cannot rely on a total word recall. A study of symbols in sequence should always begin with the kinesthetic mode through tracing followed by reproduction from memory. The *last* step in the development of the automatic use of symbols is always the paper and pencil stage.

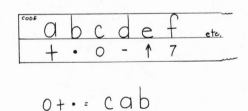

Pipe cleaners or clay can be a most valuable tool as the child forms his own letters to reinforce the spatial differences in commonly reversed letters such as *b, d, p, q.* Provide a strong, associative clue to the identification of the letter being formed, not only for its shape, but for its sound and/or name, as desired. The child forms the letter copying the symbol model while he says its sound or name.

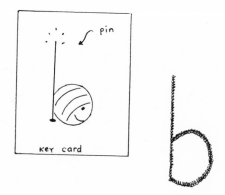

Guidelines for the spatial orientation of letters in relation to each other can be inscribed on individual chalkboards, on special writing paper, or on 3″ x 5″ index cards. The model from which the child copies should have the guidelines as well as the paper on which he copies the word. He begins by placing plastic or cardboard letters on the form then copying with his pencil (always matching to the model). Add the picture clue. An associative picture clue should *always* be added to insure meaning, thus boosting recall wherever symbols are used.

Remove guidelines from both model and paper, and practice as above to insure the child is truly aware of the spatial relationship of letters and is not relying on the lines.

Make a set of "configuration cards" on 4½" x 8½" tagboard strips as illustrated. Hold up the letter side which contains the scrambled letters of a word. Have the children copy these letters (check for accuracy). Now show them the configuration side and say, " If you unscramble your letters correctly they will make a word. Follow the pattern from left to right."

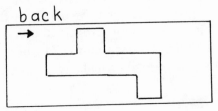

At first it may be necessary to (a) draw complete lines around (between) each letter or (b) provide cut-out letters that will fit exactly into the spaces.

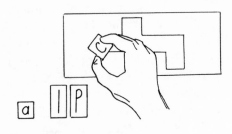

PLACE VALUE IN MATH

Manipulation and association with math is an important ingredient in helping the child *see* and understand place value, which involves sequencing and spatial relationship. Place value is a basis for much work in math and remains a problem to most perceptually impaired students who make "careless mistakes" of directionality such as reversing two place numbers, 51 - 15, or "carrying" the wrong part of the number when regrouping.

Introduce the place value "families" as being always composed of the unit which includes a one (child), a ten (mother), and a hundred (dad).

Using the "mail route" key card illustrated, introduce structure and sequence of place value with the following story: "The mailman *must* follow his assigned route (arrow shows direction) and stop at *every* house to record the number of items he leaves *each* member of the family. If he leaves no item, he must record a zero (0) for that member. The comma between families represents the gate he opens as he visits each house."

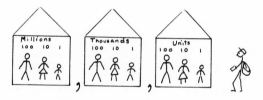

Introduce and use the following flash keys to reinforce automatic visualization of position, size and composition of unit or family (at appropriate grade level).

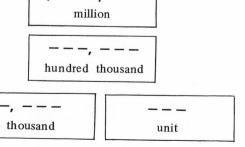

Present numbers, verbally at first, then in written form in words (one hundred fifty-six). Have the children write the number (as illustrated) as they hear it dictated; it may be a simple three place number, or as large as the children can handle.

200	"two hundred,
40	forty,
5	five."
245	then write number in full by adding.
10,000,000	"ten million,
700,000	seven hundred thousand,
52	fifty-two."
10,700,052	then write number in full.

As the next step, have the children build the number by writing each part over the one below as illustrated.

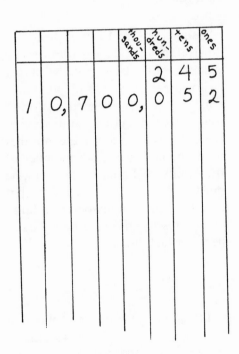

It may be necessary to structure the work paper with a visual static reminder so that auditory/visual match is more accurate. By placing a sheet of lined notebook paper on its side, a place value key can be made and numbers as outlined above written in appropriate columns.*

*It is essential that children are aware that the reason, thus the need, to write their numerals under each other correctly is that many errors are made because of placement. Complex problems are thought of as too hard because of lack of awareness of structure. A guide can be provided by turning a sheet of lined paper sideways, or by making special math paper . . . page 43. This is an effective visualization for the reinforcement of placement when writing problems.

NAME _____

DATE _____

MATH

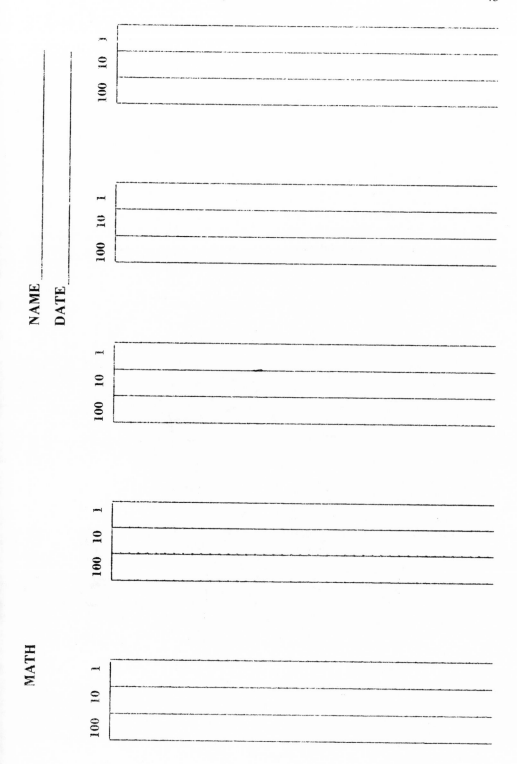

Activities such as the following two can help reinforce the child's understanding of the shift in value as a shift in position occurs.

Place  columns on board. Call off, "Write two 10's and one 1. What is the number?" The class then writes, looks, and reads. Then add hundreds, etc. as needed.

When multiplication is reached, call off multiplication facts such as, "If 4 x 5 = 20, what is 4 x 50?" Have children see that a zero added in the problem is therefore added in the answer. Class writes and says the new answer.

TELLING TIME: A SPATIAL/TEMPORAL ACTIVITY

Learning to tell time is a very complicated process involving spatial/temporal awareness or the awareness of the time it takes to span a distance. Various time intervals are assigned arbitrary terms. The child learns to visualize the use of these terms by experiencing the time intervals. We unfortunately use many of these terms loosely and in everyday conversation. For example, a minute should have a specific feel to it (time span), but we often say to the small child just learning the meaning of time referents, "I will be there in a minute." That minute can be up to any amount of time and is probably never really a minute, nor rarely the same span of time. This misuse of the labels of time intervals is true for many terms.

In addition to the terms and the feel for a span of time, we have symbol systems to be read, so that we can record time and view its representation of past, present, and future (clocks and calendars).

The calendar is one symbol system but its complexity is at least offset by the static nature of its format and the fact that we can actually mark off time on it and see the passage of days and the nearness of days. We can mark on it holidays and events and follow to see how close they come to each other and to the present. Thus, we can use manipulative and kinesthetic avenues to enhance passage of time as expressed by the calendar. The testing of our knowledge of the calendar in school is really not a measure of our ability to use a calendar to record, view, and sense the time intervals it expresses. Calendars are so commonly available that a person could carry one in his wallet and have one in every room of the house, school, and office. Thus, knowing how to read and use them should be our only concern.

Reading a watch seems to be a mammoth job for children with learning lags related to spatial/temporal awareness. Though a watch has a structured system and is visual in format, it has compacted the span called a day (24 hours) into a unit which is shown by one-hour units and read by one-minute units. In addition, the figures, at least on watches, are small and closely placed, therefore can cause reading errors. And the figures vary from Arabic numerals to Roman numerals to dots to dashes. There is no form constancy to guide rapid recognition. Once read, the figures must be held in the head and visualized against a future time and the span judged. The child can count ahead and read the interval, but he must have good one-to-one counting ability and be able to do so visually rather than kinesthetically.

The terms (words) used in "telling time" are expressing spatial/temporal relationships. This relationship when reading a watch is read as " . . . past the hour," or . . . to the hour." We must learn to read the specific amount past or to the hour in quarter and half hour intervals, and in five minute and one minute intervals. To do this and to perceive its meaning and act upon it is "telling time."

If a child has difficulty learning to tell time the part of the process which is causing the problem must be identified and remediation provided. In the meantime, the associative approach should be utilized in helping him read the clock so that he can use a clock or watch as a tool to get to school on time, get home on time, etc.

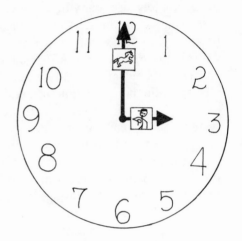

Provide a large (real) clock which has no cover over the face and provide paper plate clocks with moveable handles for each student. On the small arm or hand, place the figure of a stick figure man looking at a watch in his hand. On the large arm or hand, place a racing horse. Tell the following story to explain the reason for these figures.

"Let's think of the clock as if it were a training track for a race horse. The top of our clock, or the numeral 12 is the first starting post. Every track has to have a time keeper and a horse to run the track. The larger (or longer arm) represents the horse as he has to run all the way around the track, while the timekeeper (smaller arm) only has to clock the start and the finish of each race. To do this the timekeeper moves slowly from the starting point that marks the race to the starting point of the next race, indicated by the numerals 1 to 12. His location tells us which race is being run (which hour). The horse runs the full track (from 12 to 12) each time." (Later the children need to learn that *any* full circuit is an hour: 12:02 to 12:02, 9:54 to 9:54, etc.) "Let's watch this happen." Move the large hand of the clock slowly around from 12 to 12 and the smaller hand will automatically move properly from 12 to 1, 1 to 2, etc. Now practice until the concept of which hand tells which part of the time is solidified.

Next step and story: "Let's cheer for our horse as he runs the track and be sure to notice how far into the race (the hour) he is at all times. Start the hands moving from 12, saying, "We're off and running; now the horse is approaching the quarter-after mark, or he is one-quarter past the starting point (hour); he is now (as you continue to move the hands appropriately) halfway through the race or half past the start (hour); he is coming into the home stretch and is now three-quarters the way home or one-quarter to the finishing point (hour); and he is now approaching the finishing point. Let's see you run a race; make it race number two (2:00). Where will you place the timekeeper? The horse? Good. Run the race. When the race is over, where will the timekeeper be at the 3? Continue to run races while gradually reducing the verbiage to the correct wording of *quarter past, quarter to (of),* or *half past."*

Teach the student that we can be even more exact about where our horse is at any given point on the track. Show that the marks directly under the numerals also represent five-minute intervals. "Try to tell me how many intervals he is past or to the hour by counting by five from the starting point (12)."

Finally, introduce in the same way the reading by one-minute intervals.

Chapter 3

Laterality, dominance, and directionality

L ATERALITY and directionality are so basic to the reading process that they must be appraised and developed if the child is to have real success with symbols.

Laterality is the *internal awareness* of the two sides of the body and their difference (not the same as the naming of left/right). The use of laterality is inherent in the movements of the body for balance. It must be automatic and consistent.

Laterality leads to directionality, which is an external awareness of rightness and leftness of the relationship of objects to each other. A child may learn to respond to the words *left* and *right,* but can he do so automatically, or without checking first such clues as glancing at his right hand, and is he always accurate? If there is no internal leftness and rightness, there will be no automatic visual response to leftness and rightness outside the body, and consequently the directional differences between *b* and *d* are easily confused and at best are slow and inconsistent in being recognized correctly.

From laterality is developed a lateral dominance, or a preference for one side of the body as the lead side, while the opposite member becomes the nondominant, but supportive side. If both sides try to lead, or if automatic and rapid sequencing of movements cannot be accomplished, one cannot smoothly handle many motor tasks. If the body has not settled within itself which side will lead and which will follow, and keeps changing the lead, we say a person is ambilateral or has not established dominance. If dominance has been established where the right hand, but left eye (or vice versa), has been chosen as preferred, we say the person has crossed dominance.

Thus, before attempting to correct the directional problems the child has with symbols, a program to develop laterality by following a step-by step program must be carried through sequentially to completion. Laterality grows out of body awareness and exploration of space. If it has not developed by the time a child reaches formal learning, especially where symbols are utilized, he will experience many problems. Following are programs which are recommended for the development of laterality. These programs should be provided before or while the activities in this chapter are utilized.

Delacato, *The Diagnosis and Treatment of Speech and Reading Problems* (Springfield, Thomas, 1963), is a technical and thorough step-by-step detailed text covering concept, diagnosis, and treatment procedures related to neurological organization as developed by the Institutes for the Achievement of Human Potential in Philadelphia.

Delacato, *A New Start for the Child with Reading Problems* (New York, McKay, 1970), outlines for parent and classroom teacher evaluation and therapy in the development of hemispheric dominance toward improved reading, writing, and language.

Kephart, *The Slow Learner in the Classroom,* rev., (Columbus, Merrill, 1974), outlines evaluation techniques and recommends training for laterality development, as well as development of directionality, body image, eye/motor coordination, and visual perception.

Directional awareness grows out of laterality. Directionality refers to the knowledge of leftness and rightness of objects in relation to the body or to each other. Symbols have meaning only by their relative position, and a word is but a series of symbols arranged in a specific sequence.

The following activities are designed to help the students gain awareness of the directional nature of symbols. However, any lag or deficiency in the development of laterality or lateral dominance must be considered as the primary target and therapy must be provided, as these activities will not solve the basic cause of the errors, though they will help the child compensate during laterality therapy.

DIRECTIONALITY AND SYMBOLS

Sequential order and a left-to-right working pattern are the keys to reading and writing success. The terms *left* and *right* are not the key, nor is emphasis on the directionality of an individual symbol in isolation, though this is also of importance.

Provide objects which have obvious directionality (cars, trains, arrows, guns, etc.) and place them randomly in a line. Have the student face them all in the same direction.

Using the toys above, the teacher may place all but one in the same direction. Have the child choose the one in the opposite direction. Begin with widely discriminating objects and progress to close discriminations.

Using the same idea as above, substitute pictures of objects and repeat.

Use pictures in workbook exercises which practice the concept of directionality discrimination, and *never* have the child cross out or underline. Have him place an arrow on each picture to show its direction, as this establishes the concept of directionality.

Use a kinesthetic and associative approach for the very difficult *b* and *d* reversal problem. Print the letter *b* on a card and make on it a face like a bee. Print the letter *d* with the picture key of a dog's face and tail. Tell a story that emphasizes that when we *first* pat the dog, he *then* wags his tail.

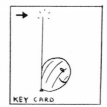

Most children do not have difficulty writing or reading the upper case *B* so its form may be employed as an associative and self-checking clue for the child who is having trouble with the lower case *b*.

Distribute mimeographed sheets with the lower case *b* and *d* in random order. Sheets will be headed with an associative clue of *B* = *b and D* = *d* and instructions, "To tell if the letter is a *b* draw in the top circle lightly. If it makes a *b* it is correct. Find and trace all the *b's.*"

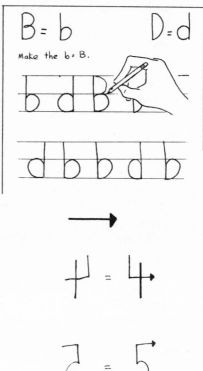

Numbers or letters that are often easily reversed may have the correct direction signalled with an arrow reminding that the hand moves from left to right and top to bottom, just as our eyes do in reading.

Left/right Progression

Picture series with few or no words should be frequently presented to children, discussed, then cut apart and pasted on firm tagboard or cardboard. These sequential frames can then be used repeatedly by children for left to right reading. Provide a numbered guide frame into which the student can place the picture series. Also provide a directional arrow at the top left-side margin.

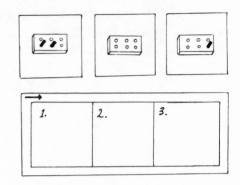

The phonetic functions of letters depend upon the letters being perceived in their right place within the word. A letter has its character as a symbol only when it is oriented in one particular way, both in the word and in isolation. Note how the letter *o* takes on different meaning (sound) depending upon (a) its placement, *on* or *no* and (b) its relationship to other letters. cow, won, coat, cot.

Geometric Forms

Place identically sized, but differently colored squares of cardboard (or use blocks) on the table in front of the child in random placement. Ask the child to place his squares in the same order as your model. Be sure he works in sequence from left to right. The model may show a series from three to eight blocks, depending upon the age and level of the student. Use an arrow at the top of the page or model to remind him of the direction in which he is to work.

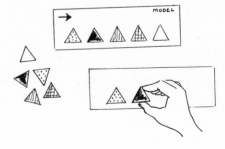

Repeat the above procedure with equilateral triangles.

Isosceles triangles are then introduced and placed in various positions.

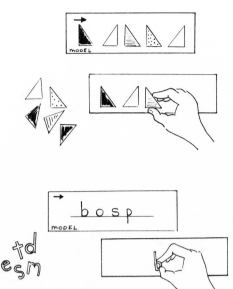

Symbols should be used next (with or without building words). Continue with a model and use a manipulative letter set.

The Alphabet

Attention to writing the child's name can bring focus on the left-to-right progression. Place a red arrow at the top left of his paper to clue him. A green (for *go*) pipe cleaner or green line down the left side of his paper adds a vivid visual clue to return and to start at the left. Begin the page with a model so that he works directly below the model.

Block out sections of a sheet of paper and number each square 1, 2, 3 for a three letter word. Present a model above the blank sections into which a letter is placed to fill the sequence and the word. Always accompany the model with a picture key. This system may be used for words in which transpositions occur. The arrow affords a further directional reminder.

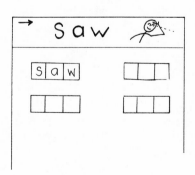

Mimeographed sheets may be employed to help the child gain reinforcement for the common transposition of words such as *no - on* and *was — saw*. The same procedure as with isolated letters is employed. The page is always headed with associative picture clue and directions are given for tracing one of the two reversible words only. Reinforcement and training must be for *one of a pair* only to establish that one thoroughly before introduction of the reverse word or symbol.

Writing letters *a, b, c, d,* in sequence is another associative clue for *b, d* reinforcement. Always begin with matching (first line) for the child to follow visually and a picture clue for the child to follow comprehensively.

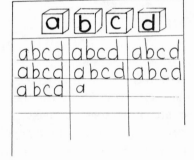

Words which are frequently transposed can begin with green (for *go*) the remainder of the letters being colored red. Tracing, then copying the word reinforces left-to-right movement of eye and hand for reading and writing.

Mathematics

Math processes are worked in a right-to-left direction, and further confusion results for the child with laterality and/or directionality problems.

An arrow used as a clue to the working direction of a problem (double column arithmetic and multiplication) can spell the difference between correct and incorrect work. A bright reminder to return to the left side of the paper will continue to reinforce the overall reading of problems from left to right.

DIRECTIONALITY AND NUMBER SEQUENCE

Too often the approach of learning to count orally and in sequence from one results in an inability of a child to come forth with a number unless he starts from the beginning every time. The response of *one more* and *one less,* which is needed for addition and subtraction, is affected, and the recognition and writing of numbers is affected.

Provide squared-off paper, ten squares across, ten down, placed in plastic sheets, and a wax marking crayon. Once a student can count and write his numbers to ten, he can begin. Put the numbers 0 to 9 across the top row as illustrated. With the teacher's help (verbal or visual) pupils write the numbers 10 to 19 in the next row, noting that the end number (the one's place) is the same as in the top row. Continue in this manner to 99.

0	1	2	3	4	5	6	7	8	9
10	11	12	13	14	15	16	17	18	19
20									
30				34	?			?	39
?									
50	?			?	55				
?									

Wipe off the sheet and begin again with 0 to 9, adding 10 to 19, then stop. "Let's go down our paper by tens." Students fill in with the teacher as they note that the beginning number (ten's place) goes up by one. Now finish each row across to 99. Wipe clean. Begin with 0 to 19. Complete tens to 60. Skip to various squares as desired. "Put in the number. . . . What comes after? What comes before?" etc., as illustrated.

Dot-to-Dot Picture Books (1 to 10)(1 to 25)(1 to 50)

Provide a number line (1 to 25) for each child and have him follow the numbers by referring to his number line for consecutive numbers until he has completed the

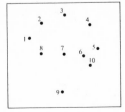

picture. At first, use only pictures going from 1 to 10; then 1 to 25.

Watch for those who cannot keep their place on the number line. If one cannot, provide a card to move along the line as he progresses.

Watch for those who cannot find the number on the dot book. If a child has difficulty, teach him to scan with his finger in a logical left-to-right, top-to-bottom search pattern.

Watch the child's control. Provide a ruler at first, if needed, or teach him to put the finger of his non-writing hand on the next dot. This kinesthetic guide seems to help a great deal.

Continue dot to dot over 25 by saying, "What comes after 5? Good. Find 26. What comes after 6? Good, Find 27 . . . " until the children see the concept and can continue without the teacher's verbal guidance.

Chapter 4

Perceptual constancy

PERCEPTUAL (visual) constancy refers to the recognition of an image as being the same image when seen again, either in the same circumstances, position, size, texture, etc., or in different surroundings at a different time.

For a person to become a fluent sight reader, he must recognize words he has learned and not have to decode the symbols he sees each and every time.

Perceptual (making meaning from) constancy (sameness), is very complex because in grouping stimuli there are many ways to group, or rather many aspects from which one must choose the part or parts which will be held constant.

A child learns to recognize Mother as unique among people and recognizes her as his mother regardless of what she wears or how she looks at that moment. He uses a set of clues and is not distracted by the fact that surrounding clues change.

At a later level he learns labels for his environment and can accept that a chair is a chair no matter what its size, shape, color, or placement. He makes this judgment by its function.

When he enters school and works with the world of symbols, he learns that symbols also keep the same label in different sizes, compositions, colors, and even shapes. A, a, *a*, *a* are still the letter *A* and was, Was, WAS, *was* are still *was*.

Suddenly the child encounters symbols that do *not* keep the same label if *position* is changed: *b/d/p/q, was/saw,* etc. And further, the position of symbols in relation to each other alters their constancy of meaning (sound), for example: *mat, mate, maul, mar, warm.*

The symbols representing number values are much more constant than letters, so that this may be one reason many children learn to handle math, yet remain poor readers.

A child learns words, which at first he recognizes by outside shape,

then he learns that many words can have that shape but are not the same.

Now he has to look for minor, more discrete differences in order to recognize sameness or constancy. The child who guesses by initial clue or by sameness or overall shape has not moved far enough along in development of perceptual constancy to see the finer likenesses and differences and become a reader.

This ability must become very refined if he is to handle the symbols for our language. In helping him gain this ability, a step-by-step developmental program is outlined in this chapter.

DISCRIMINATION OF FORMS

Grouping According to Shape

Provide a set of six each of round, square, and triangular shapes painted on one side so that all circles are blue, all squares are yellow, and all triangles are green. The other side of each should be painted red so that color is *not* a clue to form recognition.

Supply key cards on which are drawn a picture of each shape, one shape to a card. Turn the shapes to the consistent color cue side. Choose a key card showing one of the shapes. Have the children sort by pulling out all of that shape from the mixed set. Color is the associative aid. Have them always refer to the key card so transfer begins to be made between the three-dimensional and linear levels. Next use the side of the shapes where sorting must be accomplished by form alone despite irregular color stimuli. Use keys.

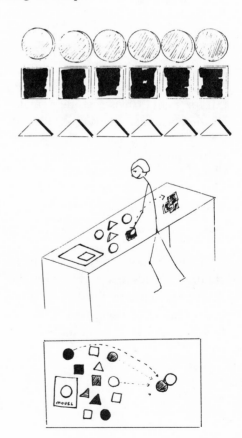

Supply another set (set B) made as previously described, but of ovals, rectangles, and star shapes. Mix with the first shapes (set A). Supply key cards for the new set. Progress from the distinctly different shapes to sorting of successively less readily distinguishable shapes. Use same procedure as previously used.

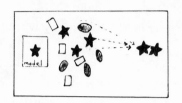

Supply a set of shapes color coded as in set A, using forms as closely related to letter shapes as illustrated. Mix this new set with sets A and B. Now sort as previously instructed.

Place a set of shapes in a series, left to right. Have a student make another set just like yours. Place a set of key cards in a series, left to right. Have the student make a set like yours (with his blocks).

Make picture dominoes from children's readiness books, or make linear drawings as illustrated. Play as any game of dominoes. Progress to sets with letters and numbers.

PERCEPTUAL CONSTANCY: REGARDLESS OF SIZE

The child must recognize an object or symbol regardless of size factors that may seem to change its appearance.

Grouping According to Size

Provide a set of longitudinal strips of different width, height, and depth. Begin with two strips of widely different size. Have a child recognize "larger" and "smaller," "thicker" and "thinner," etc. Teach size variables in all dimensions (taller, wider, thicker, shorter, thinner, narrower, etc.)

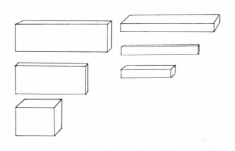

Progress to discrimination of size for two or more variables. Teach size range, first with same shapes, then with different shapes.

Provide a variety of geometric forms of the same shape but different sizes. Show one of the geometric forms. Ask the children to identify all the same form in various sizes. Thus, size constancy becomes related to shape constancy so that the two may work together as a dual perceptual aid to discrimination.

Provide a variety of letter shapes in different sizes. Repeat as above.

b b C c f f

Repeat the exercises above, but find specified shapes embedded in pictures. Follow same developmental progression as outlined.

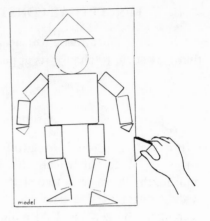

Make a page of linear forms on duplicator sheets. Repeat the procedures above. Continue to use kinesthetic/manipulative aids by having the child cut out a sample of the shape to be identified, and move it along the sheet left to right as he attempts to identify like shapes in all sizes.

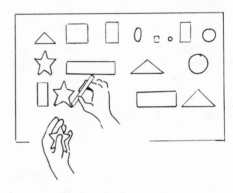

PERCEPTUAL CONSTANCY: SHAPE

Perception of Form Regardless of Size or Position

Linear level, paper and pencil exercises have a reduction of cues and should not be used until the student is ready to move past the kinesthetic learning stage. Guidance must still be given so that exercises are not test situations, but are learning/reinforcement activities.

Provide a duplicator sheet which contains a picture and its individual shapes as illustrated. Have the children cut out each shape and match it to its counterpart which is incorporated into the picture. If necessary, provide a template which can be placed over the linear form as an independent self-checking device.

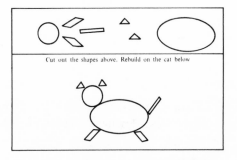

Provide pictures which are drawn out of clearly delineated shapes as illustrated. Their sizes and positions will not be constant and shapes will be embedded among other forms. Have the children color or trace the outline of each linear shape designated by a key card provided (a circle, then all squares, etc.).

Paper and pencil exercises, visual recognition with no kinesthetic clue helps us know if there is transfer of skill in perceptual constancy to the fully linear level. This is necessary before the reading and writing processes are taught as the major activities.

Provide sheets of geometric shapes where color clue is supplied as an aid in recognition of like forms. Have children trace all of a designated form (all circles, then all squares, etc.). View and work left to right and back again as in reading. They should still refer to a clue, but the clue can be a code at the top of each sheet.

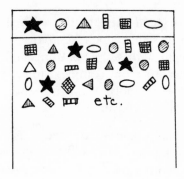

Next, provide dittos where geometric shapes are outlined bodly, but not colored. Follow the same procedure.

Reduce exterior stimuli by presenting a sheet where shapes are all in black.

Then present exercises where the forms are of fine outline, so that visualization of shape alone, as in reading, is the only clue.

Extend this practice with shapes to designs which simulate letters. Begin with simple patterns and progress to more complex, lower case-type symbols, following the steps outlined above.

The same ditto sheets as in the activities above can be utilized in developing left-to-right progression and the ability to shift from one stimulus to another needed to use the reading code.

SYMBOL DISCRIMINATION

Work in the discrimination and perception of shape constancy when extended to symbols requires a major change in perception. The child must also recognize that some letters and words are not the same in any position. For *b/d, p/q, g/q, n/u, m/w, no/on,* etc. there is an "up" and "down" and a "right" and "left," and that all symbols have a set "preferred" position. Some children cannot make this judgment rapidly in viewing the reader, and thus rely on a slow, careful process of reading, not gaining fluency or speed, but losing accuracy.

The first step in training to rapidly recognize symbol constancy must be with three-dimensional, manipulative materials.

Templates should be provided with removable inserts. Children should trace inside the template, then close their eyes and reproduce the movement on their desk. Chalk or powder should be powdered on the desk so their product can be seen by them when they open their eyes. To reinforce memory, tracing should always be immediately followed by *eyes-closed* reproduction (emulating the full traced movement).

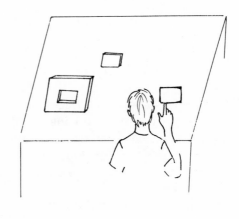

An orientation to letters requires directionality emphasis of "begin at the top of each letter, use a continuous movement throughout the letter." (The exceptions, of course, are *f, k, t, x, y,* which require two movements each.) Each template should have a green dot (green for *go*) at the starting point. Circular letters require a special directional arrow. See sample alphabet.

The template inserts can be used to trace around. Remove the template, color the letter, cut it out, and place letters in sequence, left to right, to build simple words. Always work to a meaningful model.

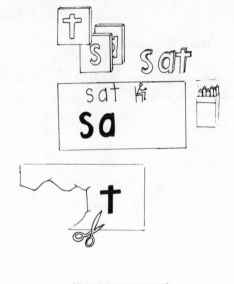

The child next progresses to the use of pipe cleaner letters (pasted on squares of cardboard). Pipe cleaner sets should be traced, then reproduced after tracing with closed eyes. Be certain to continue the green dot starting clue.

For those for whom tracing does not seem to clarify the perception of the details, clay may be utilized. Have the child form a letter using the templates as a guide. Color, texture, and mobility give him a vivid experience that aids perceptual accuracy.

Pipe cleaners (not on cards) can be formed into letter shapes, also, and used as suggested above, but these offer less tactile intensity.

Exercises in recognizing likeness and difference in symbols are found in any number of readiness or phonetics workbooks and duplicating sheets. Great care must be taken to make this linear level one of positive reinforcement rather than a trial-and-error testing experience. The directions to underline, circle, or other nonassociative instructions should be immediately ignored and replaced with tracing to accurately reinforce shape awareness. The following are test situations as conventionally set up. If the child knows which makes a pair already, they are busy exercises. If he does not, how will he find out?

Two remedial aids can be employed. One would be a key or chart for him to refer to of the pair he is seeking. Some children have difficulty following a multistimuli guide, especially if it is at a distance from his seat (as a wall chart). For this kind of child, place the single needed clue on his desk.

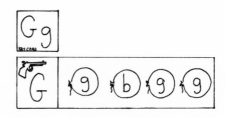

The other aid would be to have the child trace the designated symbol. This not only demonstrates that he knows his lesson, but it provides an additional kinesthetic and perceptually accurate reinforcement. In addition, a picture clue (by child or teacher) should be added to establish meaning as well as discrimination of likeness of form. Below are samples of typical workbook exercises where these principles are to be applied.

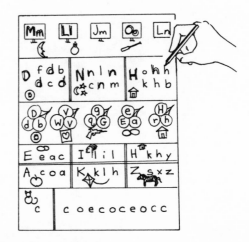

Associative Clues

To help the child with letters which continue to be troublesome because of directionality confusion *(b/d/p/q)*, the associative clue should be provided to keep at the child's desk as he works. Make a key card of the trouble letter as instructed in Chapter Three. Have the child place this on his desk as he works. Do not remove the key card until the child no longer needs to refer to it.

The words where the configuration is insufficiently distinguishing need another clue to noting *internal* likeness and difference.

Color clue can be used for words where small interior parts are the only discriminating feature. This focuses attention quickly to the important feature. Be careful to make the color clue consistent with the pattern being keyed.

MOTOR PERCEPTION AND MEMORY

To heighten visual, tactile, and kinesthetic discrimination, perception, and memory, we must develop *motor* discrimination, perception, and memory.

Make a box and cut a hole in one side large enough for a hand to go through. Place an object in the box. "Is it hard or soft? Is it round or square? etc."

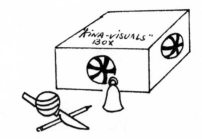

When a child has the concept and moves from the familiar to the less familiar (then to symbols) he must work to a guide or the activity becomes a trial-and-error test situation.

Place several objects in the box. Provide a key card which matches one of the objects in the box. Have the child look at the key card as he feels for the matching shape. He should be encouraged to verbalize what he sees and feels.

When the child reaches the letter identification stage, present template inserts, then progress to identification of pipe cleaner letters which are pasted on cardboard squares. Lastly, have the child identify simple three letter words (first very different words; then words similar in configuration) "written" on cards with pipe cleaners. Always have him working to a model he is viewing outside the box.

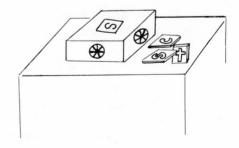

Likeness and Difference

Recognition of likeness and difference is far easier in isolation where there is no surrounding visual distraction than it is in a context such as a reader. In reading, a child must not only shift constantly from form to form, but he must recognize like form (words) when he sees it again, or he cannot develop rapid sight-reading ability. Too often teachers of a child slow in developing reading skills in context drill him harder and harder on phonics lessons. Unfortunately this may not enhance but rather further retard his slow pace.

"Kina-Bingo" is a term given by the authors to the following clinical use of the game, Bingo. Fold sheets of paper in half and in half again. Unfold and turn the other way. Fold sheet in half and in half again. When opened the sheet will be squared off in sixteen boxes. Letter in lower case letters, one to a square, on one side of the sheet. Letter in upper case letters (or numbers) one to square, on the other side of the sheet. A set of six differently arranged letters allow a small group to play bingo. Enclose each in a plastic protector and supply a crayon to each child. The teacher or student calls off a symbol or its sound, and the child must find the proper symbol and trace it. A picture clue to the sound

symbol should accompany each symbol for error-free practice.

Numbers can be reinforced in this way. Accompany by domino dot patterns. Digraphs or dipthongs can be put on the Kina-Bingo and used in the same way.

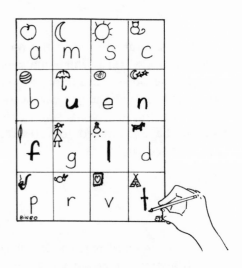

Provide ditto sheets on which are typed letters and words beginning with, ending with, or containing letters particularly troublesome to the child. At the top of each ditto sheet should be the letter to be identified and its associative clue. Instructions are given, "Find and trace this letter wherever you see it on the sheet."

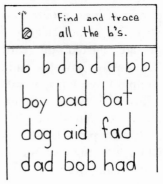

Provide ditto sheets on which are typed words for colors, for example. Use primer type size and a lot of space between lines. Place words in random order, but repeated a dozen times each. Provide a separate key card to use as a model for each of the words. Instruct the class to find and underline in the ·proper color all the places they find the word. Provide another key and proper crayon and repeat. Ditto sheets may have noncolor but similar words (animal names, etc.) interspersed. Other sheets can be made for number words or word patterns (find all the *-at* words, etc.)

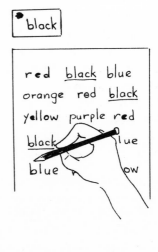

Any reader can be used in the same fashion. "Find how many times you see the word _____ ." (Specify a page or pages to scan.) Provide a key card on which the word is written or write it on the board, so the class can look it up as needed to insure accurate perceptual constancy. Work in small quantities at first (a line or two) and extend to the level of the children's current reading need.

At first, words should be easily recognized (a name, all names) and then the child can progress to the minor difference of *comes* versus *come,* for example.

At a higher level where the child handles small but not multisyllable words, provide word slips as illustrated. On each, write a word part (for compound words) or the root and common endings (*farm + er*). Have the group build words from these slips and write the total word and read it back.

The class may wish to make up words for each other, then cut them apart and play as above.

boy	scout
moon	light
farm	ing
farm	er

Word lists can be provided with instructions to "Find *in, at, ant,* etc. in these words."

WORD SEARCH   *Bob*

th**in**	planter
canter	center
w**in**ter	score
cattle	flam
th**in**k	fort
wink	small
sandle	common
scant	renew

For speed of recognition with multisyllable words the children should be directed to look at the middle (not the beginning) of a word, at its root, then at the beginning, then at the ending and combine.

department
renewal
investment
enlargement
comfortable
compartment
inhospitable
essential
unreliable
invaluable
individual
inconsistent

NUMBER CONSTANCY

A strong association between the symbol and the concrete in relation to the value of number symbols is needed. Positive meaningful practice should be established with associative approaches for error-free reinforcement.

An increase in the ability to visualize the concepts involved in the relationships of numbers can be aided by the addition of kinesthetic experiences.

Number Value

The domino patterns used on flash cards to establish a strong visualization so that these dot patterns can be used as associative clues later to make addition and subtraction facts flash cards.

Begin with buttons or similar objects to develop rapid recognition of number groups without the need to count by ones (1 to 10). By touch alone, have the child tell how many buttons he has under his hand (eyes closed). By manipulation (eyes open) have the child group and rapidly as possible tell how many buttons are before him (1 to 10).

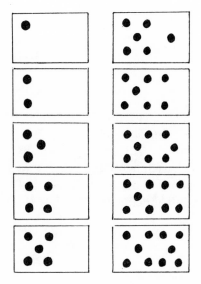

Flash fingers and let the child recognize the amount. Do not allow him to count each, but to see them as a unit. If he cannot relate this to his fingers as units, body awareness work will be needed.

Introduce domino pattern flash cards and flash for recognition of amount. Do not let the child count each dot.

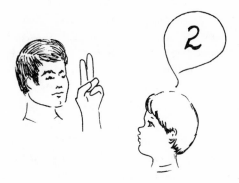

Make another set of cards of the same size and color and place a number on each from 1 to 10. Mix the domino set and the number set. Turn cards face down and in random order set out a game of concentration. Play by finding pairs, the dot pattern plus its symbol referent.

Use ditto sheets with groups of stars, lines, circles, etc. Have the child recognize number groups and label each with the correct written number. This is an important step in introducing the number symbol.

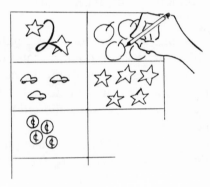

Seeing Through Arithmetic, by Scott, Foresman, and Company, has worktexts which have pages containing pictures like those above, as well as pictures which illustrate items being brought to and removed from their group. To these sets the child should place the number of each group and between his numbers place the operation sign. Thus he is introduced to addition and subtraction having formed a firm visual and symbolic association.

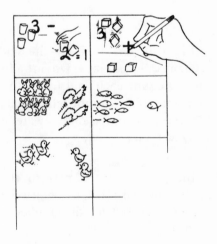

More and Less

Most children can respond to the words *more* and *less* with the correct choice of the amount of items presented. Yet, these children may be unable to hold the words and the value concept with numerical indicators because of the shift to symbol referents. Symbols for math have firm constancy (of value), especially at this level, and practice associating the symbol and a more meaningful value referent can establish number value and constancy.

Demonstrate the concept of "more" and "less" with buttons or similar objects.

Place the "more" and "less" cards, as illustrated, at the head of the table. Ask the children to match their pile of buttons to the matching key . . . depending upon the arrangement established by the teacher. "I have _____ buttons. Do you have more or less than I do?"

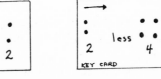

If the dots on the key card are too abstract for a student, substitute a set containing a more meaningful value clue, such as balls or apples, and then return to the dot level later. Slowly change his sentence to include the number of items held, as well as the correct more/less response. "My seven buttons are more than your three buttons."

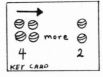
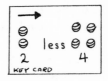

Continue to use the "more" and "less" word key cards and provide a set of dot number cards as illustrated. Have the student match these cards to the proper key which shows the sequence and then respond, "Five is more than three."

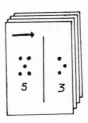

Beginning Addition and Subtraction

From the knowledge of more and less comes addition and subtraction with plus and minus one. Provide a number line with arrows and signs as illustrated below.

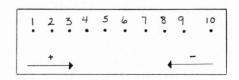

Have the children place their finger on a number. "What is one more than _____ ?" Practice.

Have the children place their finger on a number. "What is one less than _____ ?"

Now follow the same procedure, but move randomly in both directions.

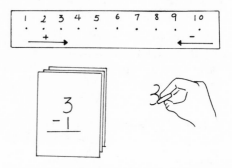

Next, provide flash cards of plus and minus one. With number bars or beads show the concept that adding can be either way, but subtracting cannot.

Have the students write each problem, using the number line as before to find and write the answer. Shuffle and do again and again until they no longer need to refer to the number line. For anyone who continues to rely on the number line, move the number line a distance away from the child so he has to get up and go to it, hold the answer, and return to his seat to finish the problem.

Many children have insufficient visualizations of the number value when working with the symbol alone. They, therefore, work by rote and will find it hard to move to subsequent steps.

"Associa-Flash Card Sets," developed and used at Educational Guidance Services, Inc. in Miami, add the associative clue, which often is *the* key to recall. The domino pattern accompanying the number provides the associative clue which can be used in building a visualization of the number value represented by the symbol.

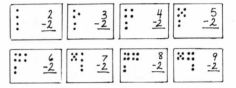

The position, as well as the pattern, is important in helping the child visualize the answer by mentally (visually) combining the dot patterns when adding or subtracting.

He must be completely familiar with the dot patterns before these flash cards are presented for use. He must not be allowed to count the dots, but must recognize (visualize) the pattern to obtain the answer.

Shuffle the cards and write each problem and its answer once each day. No key card is needed as the dot pattern is the key. Work first with plus two, then minus two, then combine the sets.

Chapter 5

Figure/ground perception

IN SIMPLE terms, figure/ground perception refers to the ability or inability to focus attention on a specific detail or details from among the many that one may be viewing at a given instant and to the ability to meaningfully see the gestalt from observation of its parts. This is occurring constantly and is probably the most important of the perceptual skills to be developed. Its underdevelopment would interfere with all other perceptual activities.

The infant uses figure/ground perception when he sees Mother as a unique and separate set of characteristics of shape, size, and texture from among the varied stimuli and images that surround and/or accompany her.

The toddler learns to find his toys, his bottle, his blanket, his furniture, etc. as unique from among the surrounding stimuli. As he gets older, if we observe, "he cannot seem to find something that is right under his nose," we might be observing poorly developing figure/ground perception. At this point we may find ourselves chiding him for lack of organization, messiness, carelessness, and not paying attention.

When this child enters a room, he may arbitrarily "tune in" to one set of stimuli without seeing it as a part of a whole, and therefore make so-called social errors. He may seem impulsive, he speaks without looking to see if anyone else is talking, he may interpret the activity incorrectly so asks "stupid" questions ("What are you doing?" when it is obvious you are sewing).

Since this child does not learn by observation he may seem inept in everyday play situations. If he is physically taken through a game step-by-step, he may immediately become able to handle it and will often be heard to remark, "Oh, is that what you do." This would tend to confirm the prior inability had been due to a figure/ground lag, as opposed to poor motivation or poor coordination.

In school, the child with poorly developed figure/ground perception would be characterized as making many "careless" errors. Careful observation might, however, show that he can work well in books with large type and clearly defined spaces between words and between lines; yet errors markedly increase with closely spaced small type (as in the transition from second to third grade readers), or he can do well with work in isolation and fail to recognize the same unit when it is imbedded in a context. Pointing with his finger or using a marker under the line as he views may markedly increase accuracy. Verbalizing as he views ("I want a red book") may increase performance as it acts as a visual focus.

It is essential that the teacher check the child's visual acuity and visual function related to fixation, fusion, depth perception, and other visual skills needed to focus on a particular spot at will and with accuracy (see glossary of visual terms). If visual function is not intact or not at a developmental stage commensurate with the skills which will be required of the child, then treatment would be turned over to a trained specialist and figure/ground perception reevaluated after visual functional therapy is completed.

If figure/ground perception is very poorly developed, the child will have great difficulty with the copy activity. To copy he must perceive the parts as they relate to the total. He may see a vague total which, when he reproduces it, has little semblance to what we can see; yet he may feel that he has copied the form adequately. In other cases, the child may see items in the three-dimensional world with ease, yet not recognize individual parts when represented in linear form. For example, a five-year-old child, when asked to color the roof of a building on a coloring book exercise, colored the entire house. When asked to point to the roof, he could not do so. A model of a house was given to him on which he easily identified the roof. The picture was again presented, but he still could not see the roof in it. How could this child be expected to learn to copy the linear set of abstract symbols that we call the alphabet?

When symbols are combined to build words, the word analysis method would require noting the pattern of symbols as they relate to each other, as opposed to focusing on one aspect. The child who calls all words from the initial clue may be unable to see the pattern, or he learns one rule and responds similarly every time he sees one particular set of circumstances, regardless of what else is present. Likewise, he may learn by rote the words *cat, mat, sat,* and fail to see that the element /at/ is present in other words and therefore transfer learning. When shown this pattern in clinical session, he usually is heard to remark, "This is easy. Why didn't anyone ever show me this?" Yet, most children see these patterns without being specifically shown.

Arithmetic processes are likewise very complex and require shifting visual (and perceptual) referents as the child works. It also requires visualizing (holding a mental image) while he works the placement of the figures. Many children who cannot grasp and/or consistently handle symbol, paper and pencil math problems, yet have good math concepts, may be experiencing a figure/ground interference.

THREE-DIMENSIONAL SORTING

Sorting of three-dimensional objects helps the child concentrate upon a particular stimuli and to shift attention when the principle of sorting is changed. "Find all round objects regardless of color or size. Find all red objects, regardless of shape or size."

Objects may be sorted for size, color, and texture, as well as for shape. The more variables in the group of objects to be sorted, the more difficult the exercise. See "Perceptual Constancy," Chapter Four.

With all figure/ground activities, the child should verbalize aloud each time to add auditory feedback, which is an aid to attention.

Show the class something that is round (a ball). Ask the children to find another round object around the room, all round objects, a round, red object, etc. Items to be perceived will vary for type, shape, size, color, texture, and complexity.

Supply boxes containing items such as assorted buttons, coins, blocks, marbles, materials, etc. Ask the child to choose the square button in a box of round buttons, the blue marble from among green marbles, etc.

Objects for Sorting

Make a box of articles all of one category, such as houses which differ only in detail. Ask the child to pick out the house with the three windows, etc.

TRANSFERRING TO TWO-DIMENSIONAL LEVEL

Provide a box of objects and identical pictures of these objects. Have the children match the picture with the object. Next, introduce pictures which are of the same object but not identical in appearance. Match.

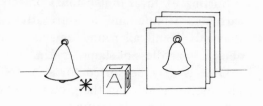

Next have a child choose an object (a ball) and find all he can (balls of any kind) in a magazine or in children's books. Have him cut them out and display them with a label ("balls").

Supply several common geometric shapes in all sizes, colors, and textures. Sort by shape. Next, find the shapes in pictures as suggested above.

Supply letter sets of various sizes, colors, and textures. Sort by shape. Next, find and trace all of one letter on ditto sheets typed as illustrated, first with each letter clearly separated from the next, then embedded in a word. Remember to always have his three-dimensional model before him as a guide.

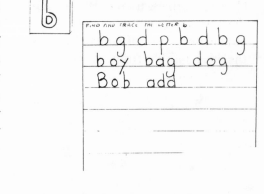

Cut tagboard into geometric shapes. Make pictures from them by pasting them on a sheet of drawing paper. This lends some depth to the picture. Have children find and color (or trace, or cut out) all the circles, squares, etc.

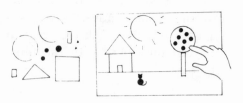

Provide cut tagboard shapes to the students. Have them paste them on a drawing paper to make their own picture. Instructions may be to use X number of circles, or they may be to make a specific picture (a tree). Children can then exchange pictures and find all the circles, etc.

FIGURE/GROUND PERCEPTION: LINEAR LEVEL

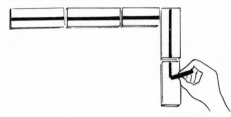

Make a set of roadways with cardboard strips. Lay them on the floor or table top. Mark out a route to follow with a colored marker. The child follows the route with a toy car.

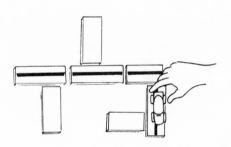

Next, lay some surrounding trails (as distractions) which must not be followed.

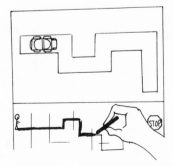

Next, provide ditto sheets with "roadways," wide at first and well delineated, later narrower and less clear, with crossing paths. Have the child follow the roadways with his toy car, then follow the roadways with his crayon.

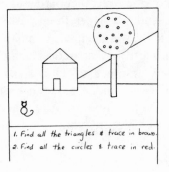

Draw pictures using geometric shapes (linear drawing) as illustrated. Children then follow the fifth activity under the heading: "Transferring to a Two-dimensional Level."

Numbers and letters can be incorporated into pictures and the principles previously outlined followed in all steps.

FIGURE/GROUND PERCEPTION: REPRODUCTION

Pegboard or other form board work involves form against a background and requires that the child not only construct a figure, but copy its position on the board. Boards should be made with nails, not holes, and use rubber bands stretched from peg to peg to illustrate a continuous line.

Provide a form board with rows and columns numbered as illustrated for each child and one for the teacher. Provide a supply of colored rubber bands to each student. The teacher initiates a line pattern noting position by numbers. The children copy by making the same line on their boards. The teacher now adds a line, the children copy, and soon a shape is completed.

Next, the teacher makes a complete form while the students watch the step-by-step process. Then they reproduce it on their boards.

Then the teacher makes a form, but does not let the class watch its execution. The class reproduces working from her model.

Provide identical pictures of easy-to-perceive familiar objects (for example, a face). One picture is to be complete in detail, the other picture is to have a part missing. Have the children complete the second picture by copying from the model.

Show pictures of familiar objects such as a face, or a common activity, such as bicycle riding, etc. and omit part of the detail (example: an eye from the face or a wheel from the bike) asking the children to find the missing detail and complete the picture. Note: To stop at the *identification* of a missing element is, in reality, testing. When a child must *complete* a picture he is kinesthetically reinforcing the total perception.

Provide a list of carefully lettered words on construction paper. Have the child draw around each word following its configuration carefully. He should then cut out the blocked word. Noting the configuration, the child rewrites the word at the right hand side of his paper, checking against the model. Place the model over his word to check size and spacing.

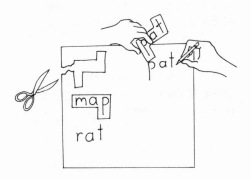

Distribute ditto sheets with block outlines at the right-hand side and words at the left-hand side of the paper. Have the child copy the words into the block configuration. Always keep left/right directionality and provide a picture clue so that the activity is meaningful.

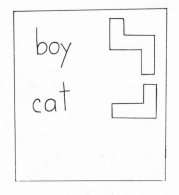

FIGURE/GROUND PERCEPTION AND MATH

Figure/ground perception is aided by color, verbalizing, knowing ahead what to look for, and increased clear space around each problem. Sometimes, just slowing the pupil's pace by pointing or underlining as he works can increase accuracy remarkably. Manipulative aids are a big help, initially.

The first time a problem with a process seems to arise is with the shift from addition to subtraction.

Obtain or cut from cardboard number bars as illustrated. There should be a set for combinations of five through combinations of ten, designed so that the bars add up when placed side by side correctly to the larger correct bar, and so that the number (symbol) is placed on each. Take the first set, ask the children to find out how many ways they can make five.

Introduce the concept that subtraction is thinking of the remaining amount when we take away part of the total amount. To establish this, give the students a problem, "Five, take away four," and have them actually move the four bars sideways and look to see what amount remains in that line. This is the answer. With a few tries the students usually exclaim with joy how easily it is done.

Now, present the students with flash cards containing the appropriate number problems for this set. Have them write each problem and its answer by using the number bars in the prescribed manner. Soon they should be able to just cover with their finger the number being taken away, and later be able to do this visually.

The next level of difficulty arises with regrouping, especially with subtraction, where too often the pupil takes the smaller number from the larger number regardless of its position in the problem. For this we offer the "egg trick." Tell the class the following story, illustrating as you tell it.

* * * * *

A young housewife wants to make a birthday cake. She finds that she has only 2 eggs in her refrigerator, but this recipe says she needs 4 eggs. So, she goes to the store and buys a box of eggs (10 in a box) and takes them home, where she now has 12 eggs and can make her cake.

Now the storekeeper has only 2 boxes of 10 left, and the next customer wants four boxes for a big party she is planning. When the storekeeper is low on eggs, he has to go down the road to the farmer. The farmer sells only by the case, each with 10 boxes of 10 eggs in them. The storekeeper buys one case and returns to his store, leaving the farmer with 3 cases. The storekeeper now has 12 boxes of eggs to sell again and can give his new customer his 4 boxes.

* * * * *

Provide a key card (as illustrated) to each student to refer as he works until he internalizes and recalls the process.

Next, the multiplication process, though generally only a problem with directionality, can be complicated with so-called careless errors due to the inability to visualize two place numbers which cause transposition. (A child may know that 5 x 5 = 25 but he puts down the 2 and carries the 5 and is totally unaware of so doing.) Expanded notation in new math tried to correct this problem by working with the entire number in a separate column, but too often children cannot transfer back to the "short" process because there is a poor relationship between placement of figures and the steps to be followed.

Take lined paper and turn it on its side. Head the paper as illustrated and place problems within the proper lines. Instruct the class to verbalize as they work and to place the full number at the right-hand side of the problem. (See example.)

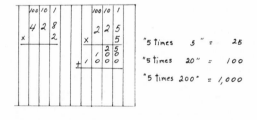

When a child has the concept well established, suggest that he can work the problem a shorter way by "holding" part of each number at the top of the column (use a circle to contain it), and adding as he goes. He must continue to verbalize and to note the figure obtained at the right-hand side.

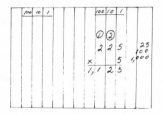

Two-place (or more) multipliers cause even greater problems with figure/ground perception because of the multitude of numbers "held." Color coding may be needed. Provide three colored pencils, such as black, red, and green. Write the problem using a color each for ones-place, tens-place, and hundreds-place figures. Work the problem as suggested in the previous exercise, but use the appropriate color pencil while doing all of the figuring with the ones-place multiplier. Now switch to the tens-place color while figuring with the tens-place multiplier.

The division process is often a real problem because of the need to shift from division, to multiplication, to subtraction, and back again. Children with figure/ground problems often have difficulty shifting. The same concepts as used with multiplication can help. Use the lined paper turned on its side and the column headings for 1's, 10's, and 100's. Place the problem on the paper appropriately. Now the pupil can verbalize as he did in multiplication (though in reverse) saying, 400 ÷ 2 = _____ and place the entire answer at the top (zeros, too). Now he multiplies, 200 x 2, and brings down the answer of 400. He must next subtract. The key at the top of his paper reminds him of the three-step problem. Another important part of this process is to return and divide, *not* to the original problem, but the remainder, saying 36 ÷ 2 = _____ , etc.

When the pupil reaches fractions, he may grasp the basic principles easily, yet not be able to handle paper and pencil problems when mixed fractions are utilized. A three-step process is used. He must again talk his way through the problem and give himself a visual association for the concept of re-grouping into like fractional units.

Write the problem and visualize what it says with pies as illustrated. See if the pieces cut are of the same size, explaining, "I would be very unhappy if you get one large piece while I get one small piece, so you must give us equal size pieces."

Therefore, the child must choose which fraction can be cut into smaller units ("we can't paste pieces back together once cut"), so that both pies have pieces of the same size. He then does this with his pencil.

Now read the new fraction and write that problem to the right hand side of the pies. Add (or subtract).

Chapter 6

Motor development

M OTOR development plays a major role in perceptual development. There is little remaining dispute that motor activities provide the basis of our awareness of space/time and shape/size, among other things; and motor development forms the percepts and concepts about our environment. The infant and toddler learns about his environment by moving through it. His movements provide knowledge of size, distance, shape, and position in space that later he is able to make from vision alone.

The benefit of movement to learning is recognized and is utilized in the multitude of available kinesthetic teaching approaches and aids. However, we may forget that

(1) the entire body needs to investigate our world, not an arm, hand, or fingers alone; and

(2) the kinesthetic avenue must be well enough developed to be a fruitful learning tool.

Gross motor activities involving the musculature of the body or large portions of it should be involved even in the task of drawing (hence writing); yet we too often teach the child to write at a table, using near point vision and finely lined paper requiring small finger movements, or at most, movement of the wrist and hand.

A kinesthetic approach to increasing accuracy of visual perception assumes that the motor movement will make the child more aware of the details of a form. Again, too often minimal movement is utilized, so little discrimination of form can be obtained, and the approach is not the help it was hoped.

Physical education and art classes, as well as planned activities in the classroom, can be balanced so that they structure training. The child must be carefully observed. When he is using his body or large muscles to execute an action, it is not a single nor simple action we are seeing. Does he have internal awareness of the two sides of his body (laterality — see Chapter Three)? If not, he may do poorly with activities requiring balance. Does he have good rhythm or smooth rapid sequencing of movements? If not, he may do poorly in synchronized or coordinated activities (such as bike riding). Does he have good eye/motor coordination (eyes guiding hand or foot)? If not, he cannot bat the ball, catch it, nor throw it well. Does he have good body awareness? (See Chapter One.) If not, he may be seen as a "clumsy child."

Since remediation should match the need, the part of the action which is not operating fully must be determined. Once determined, there are many excellent programs available. See the "Chapter Reading Reference" for an annotated listing.

SMALL MOTOR: EYE/HAND COORDINATION AND PERCEPTION

Art classes can be made a very valuable period because the multisensory, kinesthetic activities, high motivation, and approach inherent in arts and crafts can be used to advantage to strengthen large and small muscles, build perception, improve visual/motor coordination, heighten conceptual and perceptual awareness of part-to-whole relations, and aid in developing better body schema and tactile awareness.

The child may use his hands and fingers in buttoning, opening and closing of snaps and zippers; lacing and tying are excellent finger exercises which are incorporated in the use of or manufacture of doll clothes or puppet making. Be certain the items are large enough for easy manipulation of desired parts. Reduce size and complexity slowly until at the required level.

Lacing and handling yarn, then string (larger first, then of smaller diameter) may be incorporated into a variety of arts and crafts projects such as weaving, and making pot holders and sewing cards. Supply shoe laces for stringing because the finished tips make the activity easier.

Blow Down and Pick Up is a fun game. Fold pieces of paper in half so they stand when set up, then blow them down. Groups or pairs can make a game of this activity.

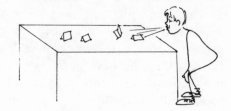

Playing cards may be laid on the table in an overlap pattern, then flipped to the reverse side.

Playing cards may be built into pyramid houses, then blown down.

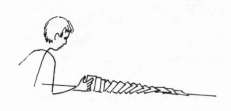

Dealing and holding cards can be utilized in the many academic helping games commercially available. Many fun card games for children can supply this small muscle activity, as well as heighten concentration, attention, visual matching, and recall.

Buttons or beads may be used in stringing activities. Materials and hole size should be large at first, then decreased slowly in size as small muscles are able to handle them.

Keeping in mind that motor activities serve to help us learn about our environment and thus develop perception and concepts, combine activities to develop the ability to follow color, shape, size, and sequence patterns.

Stringing Beads

Begin with simple patterns where one variable (color) only is changed. For example, string three round blue beads, three round red beads, and alternate three round

blue beads with three round red beads, etc. Instructions may be given orally, but an actual model should be supplied for the child to check with as he copies.

Next, the number sequence may change, first in a pattern sequence, later with no pattern, for example: 3, 2, 3, 2, etc., and then 3, 4, 2, 5, 2, 2, etc.

Next, shapes only can vary, for example: three red squares, three red circles, etc.

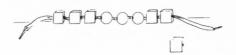

Now, more than one variable can change at one time, for example: three red squares, two blue circles, etc. Each step in stringing of beads is to become more complex visually, and thus requires attention, coordination, and the ability to shift.

Cutting

The simplest cutting exercise is the cutting of a fringe from a piece of paper or cutting off corners. Cutting light weight cardboard may be needed initially if the child's control is poor. This provides sufficient resistance so that the child is more aware of the feel and is forced into a slower pace, so fewer overcutting errors result.

Next, cut along lines with various angles. Provide heavy and thick guidelines at first.

Cut figures with curved lines.

Cut complex figures with combined angles and curves.

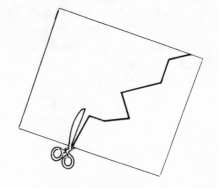

Finally, if appropriate, cut letter shapes and build words.

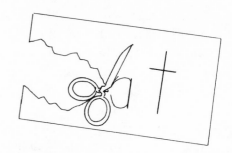

Placing and Pasting

Many small items such as buttons, toothpicks, and beans can be placed and pasted onto construction paper in a pattern to form pictures, designs, or letters. Outlined forms should be provided into which the child must place and paste specified items. This way he develops the ability to follow a pattern and stay within guidelines.

Toothpicks or Popsicle sticks can be placed and pasted into patterns on a sheet of construction paper to form a picture of a person, or object. At first, a mimeographed pattern should be provided; later, construction should be from a model.

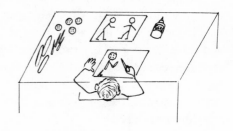

Paper shapes may be cut out and pasted into specific matching areas on a mimeographed sheet or in a commercially available book of this type of activity.

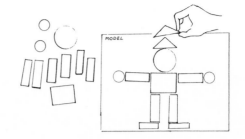

Using a hole punch, make holes in colored paper. The punched-out dots are then collected and used in pasting onto a pattern. Letters or pictures may be filled in with these tiny dots. Extremely fine finger coordination is necessary to do this.

Construction: Part to Whole

Erector sets composed of shapes involve small muscle development, as well as the ability to build a whole out of parts. The children should experiment freely at first for the feel of the pieces. Soon they should be asked, "Try to build a plane, a house, etc." Some may require a model to work from; others may need to be shown the piece as it is constructed (they cannot visualize whole to part); and some may need the teacher to verbalize them through the manu-facturing process ("Find a square. Find a triangle and place it on a top edge of the square for the roof," etc.).

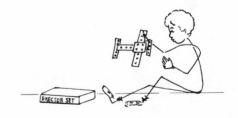

Toothpicks or Popsicle sticks can be utilized by the student in building a three-dimensional scene such as a house, fence, bird cage, etc. Here, construction again requires adequate perception of the object to be constructed so a model may be needed.

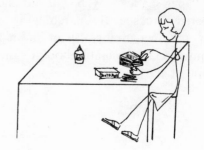

Assembly of models from simple kits is a meaningful part-to-whole situation. It requires following a linear model; thus it is an advanced perceptual activity.

SMALL MOTOR: EYE MOVEMENTS

Steps must be taken in helping the eyes function in the strict rhythmic movements required in reading, as well as in the ability to focus accurately and rapidly at a desired spot.

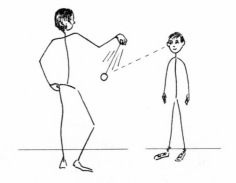

Have the child stand squarely balanced on both feet holding his head still and erect while focusing straight ahead at eye level at a button or similar ornamental object. Slowly move the object in a horizontal line on the child's eye level about twenty inches in front of him. Begin at extreme left and extreme right and move toward the center until the child can identify the object. Make a game of quick object identification of changing items, being careful that the child moves only his eyes. Repeat for vertical vision.

Following the basic procedure outlined above, use a ball on a string on which letters are written. As the ball swings inward, the child calls off the letter he sees.

Write numbers from 1 through 15 in random order on a cardboard in three columns spaced vertically about six inches apart and horizontally about twenty-four inches apart. Have each child in turn stand about five feet from the board, balanced with equal weight on both feet, head erect and stationary. Tap rhythmically with a pointer at each number in left/right sequence (as in reading) while the pupil calls off the number in time with the taps.

Initially, have him point at the number as you tap and while he says the number. In this manner, the eye movements are reinforced by motor activity, auditory clues, and association of eye/hand movement.

Following the above procedure, make charts with capital letters, lower case letters, then simple two-letter and three-letter words. Regardless of the chart used, the placement of symbols (new chart) should be periodically changed so that vision, not rote, is required in executing this activity.

Tracking can be done with a flashlight in a darkened room and aids attention as well as following a moving target visually.

Step 1.   Seat children at desks before the chalkboard in a darkened room. The teacher takes a position behind the group to observe their responses and encourage attention and accuracy during the activity. Using a flashlight, the teacher begins at the left side of the chalkboard and directs the light in a line toward the right-hand side of the board, then back, then forth. The children are to follow the light path with their eyes and with a pointed, elevated arm and finger. It is of extreme importance that each child follow the light with his full arm to establish a kinesthetic/visual connection and to insure that he is actually following the light path.

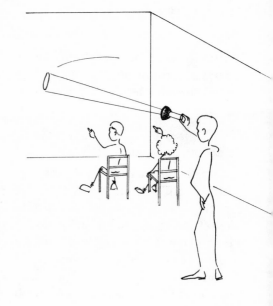

Stop the light at various un-expected places to see if the children stop their hands at the correct location. It will frequently be seen that a child continues the pattern or anticipates instead of actually attending to the track.

The path should then vary from straight to peaking patterns and curving patterns, as well as vary in speed. The path must always be from left to right or top to bottom, as in writing.

Step 2. When the children's attention is established for the direction and speed of the light, they can begin to follow symbol patterns. The teacher still begins at the left-hand side of the board and moves the light in a pattern which forms a symbol properly. The children must follow the pattern with their arms, as well as with their eyes, as before. It is thus possible for the teacher to visualize the eye movement and the attention level of the pupils and to see where an error is being made. When the light has completed the pattern of the letter, the students call out what was made. The teacher does not tell ahead of time what he is going to flash. In this way, interest and attention are better held.

Step 3. At this stage pupils are issued a piece of newsprint and a marking crayon. Instead of tracking with the arm in the air, the pupils now follow the track using their

crayon on the paper. It is important
that they do not look at their
paper, but that they follow the
light with their eyes while moving
their hands from the message received from the movement. The
teacher should return to simple
Step 1-type movements to establish
the attention and coordination of
eye and hand movements. Next, the
teacher should form geometric patterns, then return to letter forms.
Time spent should be about five
minutes per session.

Each time, the child does not
look at his tracing until the entire
pattern is formed. The teacher can
see where correction should be suggested. It will be observed, and
should be corrected at this time,
that some children use restricted
movements, lose the direction, or
anticipate.

Step 4. Words can now be formed
with the light on the board. Have
the children follow with their hands
in the air as in Steps 1 and 2. Have
them guess at the end of the track,
rather than letter by letter.

EYE/HAND COORDINATION AND CROSSING THE MIDLINE

In addition to smooth, accurate movements and the ability to focus on a given target, the eye must learn to signal the body or a part of the body and have it move to a specific spot at a given moment in time. We are two-sided individuals who can move parts of our body in isolation one time and in coordinated movements another time, but some of us cannot seem to move across the midline of our body. Thus, we switch hands, turn our bodies aside, or move the materials so we do not have to do so. This can cause us to sacrifice speed, to put our eyes at a disadvantage, and create reversals.

Many activities similar to the one presented below can be utilized, but always keep in mind the need to position the child so the target or material is at the midpoint of his body and movements must be made on all sides and above and below a "central spot."

Materials

> 1 plastic ball hung on a string from the ceiling
> rolling pins painted with three-color stripes

Procedure

Step 1. Mark an *X* on the floor where the child must stand. Instruct him that he *must* stay on his individual "spot," holding the rolling pin in front of him *in both hands.*

Step 2. The teacher swings the ball toward a child who must try to hit the ball with a particular color as called by the teacher. He must not step off his spot to do this; thus he is forced to work on both sides of his midline.

Step 3. Each time he moves off the spot or misses the ball, the teacher receives a point; when the child does it correctly, he gets a point.

Activities utilizing a balance board do not allow the child to move away from the midline (or he will probably fall off the board). Two examples follow, and there are many more such activities among the programs listed at the end of the chapter.

Catch and throw a ball while standing on the balance board.

Follow a swinging target with eyes while. pointing with extended arm.

EYE/HAND COORDINATION AND VISUAL FIXATIONS

All the following activities are to be executed in approximately the same manner. The main consideration in developing eye/hand coordination and visual accuracy is the use of a *guideline*. The idea is similar in concept to the one used by bowlers, i.e. fixing the eye on a particular spot or position and throwing at or over that spot. With all of the following activities, a line of tape, string, chalk, or whatever would be appropriate in the physical set-up should be placed from the *player to the object he is trying to reach*. For example, in Ring Toss, the line is drawn from the player to the peg. Instructions to the child are: "Move your arm forward along the line as the ring will go where your hand points." It may be necessary to practice initially moving the hand along the line with the fingers pointing in the direction of the target before the child actually throws anything at the target. This is because many children have trouble concentrating on two factors simultaneously (pointing and throwing).

As accuracy develops, move the starting point of the line further away from the child (toward the target). *Be sure the child uses his dominant hand and does not switch hands.* (Mark the back of the proper hand in some way as a clue to both teacher and child.)

These games are to be used in progressive order.

Ring Toss
    The game is played with peg and quoit and can be purchased in a children's toy store or sporting goods store; it is played as designed plus instruction given above.

Horseshoes
    A full game is available in children's toy store or a sporting goods store.

Erasers in the Basket
    If game equipment is not available, a classroom wastebasket and classroom erasers can be substituted and make a game of shooting baskets. At this point, the target can be elevated by moving the basket on top of a block, chair, or table. Do not do this until the child has developed skill in following the guideline along the ground. The guideline is continued on the floor, but the child has to elevate his arm for height.

Chair Ball
    1. A kick ball can be rolled down the aisles in the classroom, under chairs, etc.
    2. Chair ball should be used for eye/foot coordination in the same manner except it is kicked down the guideline toward the goal.

Golf Putting

Golf Balls, paper cups, and plastic putters make a more difficult level of eye/hand coordination as the line of vision is removed from the hand by the length of the putter handle.

Darts

This is an advanced step as any guideline is farther removed since the dart must fly through the air. Continue to emphasize, "the arrow should end up where the hand is pointing."

WRITING READINESS

Eye/hand control exercises form the first steps in writing readiness.

Coloring

Provide a slanted surface on which to work. This can be done with prepared boards as illustrated, or by placing an eraser under the child's notebook. Writing readiness should always be initiated on a slanted surface because "upness" and "downess" have proper meaning in this position; and control, as well as perception, is increased. Present children with a variety of mimeograph sheets containing various geometric figures. Progressive sheets present smaller figures. Provide templates or stencils that enclose each shape.

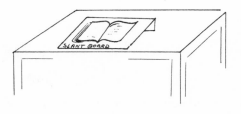

Have the children color, first with crayons, later with pencil, with up and down strokes, working from left to right inside each figure. Use the template at first to help the child stay within the limits of the design.

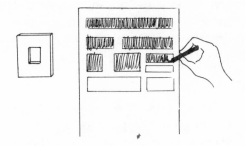

Have the child trace with a crayon around a simple (later more complex) picture of individual objects (later multiple scenes), then color it using vertical strokes in a left-to-right direction.

The next step is to establish horizontal strokes in a top-to–bottom direction.

Lastly, the child should color as the contour of the picture indicates.

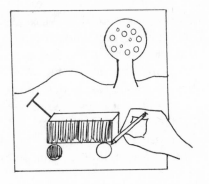

Tracing and coloring around letters leads the child into visual and kinesthetic familiarity with the symbols for writing and reading. Have the child trace around a letter template. After removing the template he then colors in the letter. Letters traced and colored in sequence form the child's first word writing experience, as well as his first vocabulary lesson.

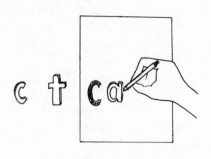

Prewriting Activity

Provide
One toy car, small, and one large paper — 16″ x 24″, or one large slateboard.

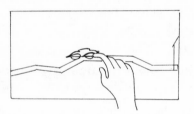

The teacher should draw a squiggly "driveway" on the paper and show the child how to drive on this driveway, pushing his car as he goes, from *left to right.*

Next, print his name in large letters on a new piece of paper. (If needed, take one letter at a time.) Take the child's hand and guide his car on this new driveway. "Let's drive on the *Paul* driveway." Teach him the correct movements (for example, if his name has a *p* say, "We must go down the driveway, then back our car up before we can go around the circle." Once he has the feel of the movements, let the child drive his driveway independently. Watch that he continues in the correct manner.

The child next tries to draw by copying his own driveway.

Transfer to writing his name without copy by referring to the model only as a recheck.

Clay can be formed by the child with guidance from three-dimensional models such as pipe cleaner letters which he can follow tactually as he constructs his clay letters. Rolling the clay into snake shapes will allow the child to form lines and circles or curves in the part-to-whole process necessary for him to understand the likenesses and differences in letters.

Clay can be pressed onto shirt cardboard and scooped out to form letters (follow a model). The child can then trace his letter and reproduce it with clay, or write it below his model with a large crayon.

Tagboard or cardboard may be used to cut out the components for forming letters (circles, stems, etc.) Rearrange the paper shapes to form letters by copying a model which has an associative picture key to the letter sound. When teaching letters, even though the primary goal is for motor control and writing skill, it is essential that the child identify meaning for the symbols. Only through meaningful sound/symbol associations will letter/motor formation offer a reliable visual clue.

MODEL

CLAY TRAY

Alphabet tracing reduces the stimuli but continues motor pattern reinforcement. Cards should be prepared with a letter in black marker pen combined with a red arrow for a directional clue. Tracing should be done with a large crayon through tracing paper. It should be followed by reproduction below while checking with the model.

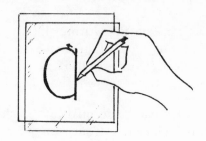

A child may write his name through the above described tracing method. His name is the most meaningful symbol to him, so these are often the first letters learned by the child. This provides sequencing and spatial relationships of letters.

Activities for writing must extend from letter formation to word formation. Many children have trouble with the spatial orientation for words. Often we see pupils who seem to have no meaning for the spacing of letters within or between words, even though they may be able to read the words.

Provide a set of alphabet cards to each child and one for the teacher as illustrated. Provide blocked-off paper onto which the card set will fit.

The teacher builds a word with letters in proper sequence *and* proper spatial orientation. The students copy the word with their letter set on their papers using the same left-to-right sequence and spaces.

Next, the teacher writes a word, but continues to fit each letter properly into the boxes. The children build with their letter set.

Then the teacher writes a word and the children copy with a pencil.

Lastly, provide unlined paper and proceed through the above steps.

Whole words can be built with tracing, coloring, and cutting letters to help emphasize form and details for writing, spelling, and reading.

The pupils and the teacher choose the proper letters to form a word. Letters are laid out in proper sequence and discussed.

Children trace each letter in sequence onto the top portion of an 8½" x 11" construction paper and replace each letter as they work.

Children color each letter in sequence to heighten the awareness of the shape.

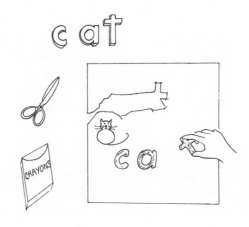

Children cut out each letter in sequence with care not to destroy the sheet.

The colored, cut-out paper letters are then to be pasted in sequence (copying original letter model) on the bottom portion of same construction sheet.

Associative picture is to be added to insure meaning for the word.

Commercially available primer or first grade paper is not recommended for children with perceptual problems. The red and blue lines of some, the dotted lines of others, and the lack of clearly defined, meaningful spaces between lines is a problem to the child with a perceptual or eye/motor lag.

A segmented or "ball and stick" method of forming letters should *not* be used as it created problems for the child with perceptual or eye/motor lag. For example, a child with a motor problem might write ⊃ as φ , while a child who tended to make reversals might write it as ⊃ .

THE PRINT STAGE
FOR FIRST AND SECOND GRADES

Copying and writing words several times is a common classroom practice. Unfortunately, children with perceptual, motor, or attention deficiencies tend to copy incorrectly, or copy accurately at first, only to lose details and accuracy on subsequent rewrites. Since this causes reinforcement of errors, it is not a desirable activity.

Tracing has long been used as an alternate to increase accuracy and awareness of the shape and details of words. By tracing over the original copy there is less chance of error. For many, tracing alone has not effected recall to a sufficient degree, especially for the abstract symbols and words of our language. A Pictogram® step added to the familiar VAKT (visual/auditory/kinesthestic/tactile) method is the *associative* link to heighten meaningful recall for words. By the addition of a meaningful picture clue, not only is the sight recognition improved, but meaning vocabulary is more accurately developed and lessons in penmanship become lessons in learning to read, to write, to spell, and to give meaning to the words.

Letters are best taught in context (in words) and *not* in isolation. It is the space/size relationship and the sequencing of the symbols that causes trouble for children with perceptual, motor, or attention problems.

In addition, some children cannot transfer what they learn in an isolated and structured exercise to use where they have to shift constantly from one symbol and sequence of symbols.

Associa-pictograms

The use of associative word pictures was introduced by Mrs. Frances McGlannan, at the McGlannan School in Miami, Florida, and has proven itself an effective technique to improve writing, reading, and spelling skills.

Clearly print a word on the board, being certain to provide bold, correctly formed and spaced letters. Use letters (and words) the child currently needs and will use daily.

Teach the child to observe accuracy of spacing, of size, and of movement from top to bottom, left to right, as he copies a word with a red pencil or crayon, onto an 8 1/2″ x 11″ sheet.

incorrect   *correct*

dOg   dog

Went   went

PaPer   paper

Remember that the children with more slowly developing eye/hand control may make many errors with a conventional segmented form of printing. These errors virtually disappear when letters are formed in a continuous movement.

Children with poor directionality awareness and habits *must* form symbols properly left to right, top to bottom, or their transfer to cursive will be difficult. Thus, the "ball and stick" approach is to be discarded.

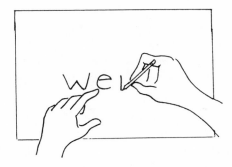

Have a child use his finger, if needed, to keep his (imaginary) line level as he moves from one letter to the next. If control or perception is very poor, the teacher should print the word on his sheet for him (or provide dittoed sheets ready for classroom use).

With guidance from the teacher, the children think about the word and draw a picture to express its meaning. The picture must be placed at the top left of the paper.

The children now are asked to trace their word three times with a fat crayon *while* saying the whole word. They should concentrate on the total word during the tracing. (Many young or problem learners will stop and talk in the process, will try to say each letter, or will trace each letter three times). Directionality must be carefully watched and correctly enforced. An arrow may be needed by some problem circular letters, such as *a, o,* etc.

Children then turn their paper over and write the word *(with his eyes closed).* If they falter or are inaccurate, they must return to the tracing step until they can write the word from recalling the feel of the movements.

Two to five new words a day can be introduced. The word sheets should then be filed in a manilla folder or notebook and be reviewed at the end of each week as an *eyes-closed* spelling/writing test. The meaning of each word can be checked by asking the children to add the pictogram next to each word (from memory) on their test sheets. Words that are recalled with ease can be tossed away dramatically to build a feeling of achievement.

Pictograms must be used properly to be of benefit. The key to recall may be the vivid or even unique association, in picture form, which is brought to the word *by the child.* The clue must be *his* clue. The association must be meaningful to him. With words which are easily visualized and concrete and which he can learn through a phonetic analysis approach, this method may be time-consuming without sufficient benefit. To use pictograms with words which are less tangible makes the child search for a key to open the door to recall. Once he opens the door himself by finding the proper key, he will be more likely to remember how the next time he approaches it. If we open the door for him, how will he know how to do so himself the next time?

Eyes-closed writing requires a true internalizing of the feel of the form and the movement and is a *must*. Children must not be allowed to look back at the word after tracing, as they are then using immediate visual imagery instead of motor memory. Motor memory requires concentration which intensifies intake. Eyes-closed (or look away) writing, instead of conventional "watch the line" is essential for speed. Can you drive a car or type if you have to look to see where your feet and hands are? You cannot use writing for note taking or communication if the penmanship is taught as a visual skill.

KINA-WRITING: GRADE THREE THROUGH ADULT, CURSIVE STYLE

The key to writing and reading in cursive is the establishment of an association between the printed and the cursive word. Through a step-by-step kinesthetic/associative approach, the child learns to conceptualize and visualize the cursive process *as the printed form connected.* In addition, the associative pictogram aids recall of sight vocabulary, spelling, meaning vocabulary, and foreign language vocabulary. Kina-writing was developed and named by the authors and has been used at Educational Guidance Services, Inc. with success since 1967.

Take words from any book in which the child is working which requires recall reinforcement. At first, avoid words with an *r, s, f, z.* These are the only letters which change from the printed form to the cursive form. Provide white, unlined tagboard cut into 4 1/2″ x 11″ strips.

Copy each word, one word to a kina card in red pencil. Proper and exaggerated spatial relations are needed to fully involve the child kinesthetically and to heighten his perception of the word configuration. (Copy about five words per lesson.) Check for accuracy of copy and letter formation.

Draw a picture on the back of each card to illustrate the meaning of the word. Teacher or parent must check at first for correctness and accuracy of meaning. Thinking—who, what, when, where, why, how—helps the student make his pictogram fully meaningful. Keep the pictogram simple, but accurate.

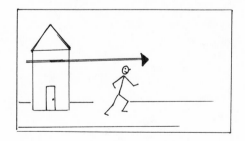

Discourage extraneous details which are not needed to provide meaning.

Connect each letter using a dark crayon, so the finished word appears in cursive form. (At first the teacher illustrates on the board using two chalk colors.) Careful guidance is needed at this step where directionality and eye/hand coordination problems may interfere with the child's execution of this stage. (Check before tracing.)

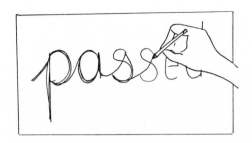

The instructions given in introducing the connective step are. . . "Swing up to where the letter begins when you print _p_ . (Note that it is often necessary to correct the child's directionality by placing an arrow to remind him that all letters move from left to right as they are formed, and that we begin at the *top* of each letter. Segmenting manuscript letters is detrimental to the child with directional or eye/hand coordination problems.) "Make your letter as always, _p_ swing up to the next letter _pa_ make _pa_ etc." Always teach with words, never as letters in isolation.

Have the student trace a word three times with a crayon as he says the word quietly, but aloud. (Be sure he keeps his arm from resting on the table. Freedom of movement as well as large movements is important.) Then he should turn the card over and write the word on the chalkboard or scrap paper with eyes closed. Check to the model. Have him retrace it if it is incorrect. Do each word in turn.

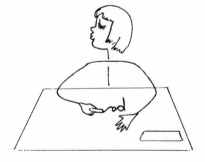

File words in a shoe box, in *abc* order, for use as flashcards and vocabulary review and spelling builders. About every two weeks have students test each other by calling off the words from the box and writing them, eyes closed. All words written correctly are discarded. Words still difficult should be reviewed for appropriateness and/or given in another format.

When writing is extended to sentences, spacing can again become a problem; one word may blend into the next or spaces within a word be uneven. Reading back what is written can be very difficult.

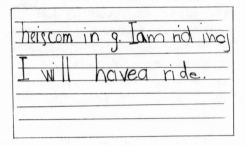

Divide off sheets of paper with strips of Scotch tape® so that the length of the words to be used can fit comfortably within the sections. Provide sentences to be copied. The students write each word of the sentence within the space and the Scotch tape forms an effective, yet invisible barrier to force them to leave sufficient space between the words. Thus, proper spacing is obtained, yet visual continuity of the sentence is not altered.

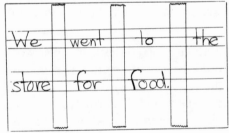

CHAPTER READING REFERENCE

Abernethy, Kathleen, et al.: *Jumping Up and Down.* San Rafael, Acad Ther, 1970.

A fully and clearly illustrated manual of motor activities to develop balance and coordination.

Banas, Norma, and Wills, I. H.: Perceptual games. In: *Open Court Kindergarten Program.* LaSalle, Open Court, 1970.

A step-by-step program of individual activities to develop perceptual/ motor efficiency in play experiences at school.

Bentley, William G.: *Indoor and Outdoor Games.* Palo Alto, Fearon, 1966.

Play activities are described for use in kindergarten through grade six. They are nondiagnostic, but are indexed by grade level expectancy.

Cratty, Bryant J.: *Movement and Spatial Awareness in Blind Children and Youth.* Springfield, Thomas, 1971.

Step-by-step development for the blind of body image, spatial orientation, large muscle control, and more. Can be readily appropriated for the perceptually impaired.

Frostig, Marianne, and Maslow, Phyllis: *Movement Education: Theory & Practice.* Chicago, Follett, 1970.

Easy-to-follow games and exercises to promote motor skills, develop body awareness and perceptual skills, language, arithmetic concepts, and other academic learnings. Includes research and theories on the importance of learning through movement.

Furth, Hans G., and Wachs, Harry: *Thinking Goes to School: Piaget's Theory in Practice.* New York, Oxford U Pr, 1974.

Contains page after page of practical activities based upon Piaget's theory of cognitive development.

Gordon, Sol, and Golub, Risa S.: *Recreation & Socialization for the Brain Injured Child.* East Orange, New Jersey Assoc. for Brain Injured Children, 1966.

Suggests how to plan and organize a therapeutically oriented recreation and socialization program within the school setting, at home, and in setting up a summer day camp and swimming program.

Hackett, Layne C., and Jenson, Robert G.: *A Guide to Movement Exploration.* Palo Alto, Peek, 1966.

Identifies goals, provides teaching techniques, and a multitude of activities to develop fitness, motor skills, mental, and socio-emotional growth.

Kephart, Newell C.: *The Slow Learner in the Classroom,* rev. Columbus, Merrill, 1971.

Presents a rationale for learning, followed by a series of techniques related to successive steps in the development of form perception, space discrimination, and time dimension, through movement.

Rowen, Betty: *Learning Through Movement.* New York, Tchrs Coll, 1963. Practical suggestions for teaching language, mastering math concepts, science and social learnings.

Chapter 7

Visual memory

VISUAL MEMORY is not a discrete skill. It is looked upon as the storage and retrieval stages in the learning process. This is an oversimplification of a very complex situation.

When we say a child has poor visual (or motor) memory, we indicate that he cannot give back to us a response that we believe him to be capable of giving. This is usually based upon the fact that we know he has the movement or image given to him at one time, and therefore we expect that he should be able to repeat it or exhibit that he recalls it in some way.

We may be told that his lack of memory is because he needs to have an experience repeated more frequently before he can remember it; drill and overexposure techniques are advocated.

We may be told that his lack of memory is because he does not pay adequate attention, so we make him keep notebooks, and write everything down, and we put him in the front of the room close to us.

We may be told that his lack of memory is lack of motivation, and we use praise, rewards, and even psychological or psychiatric counseling if a great enough problem is seen.

We find that children given certain medications suddenly exhibit improved memory and wonder if we should recommend the same treatment for others with poor memory. Conwell, in *The Role of Drug Therapy*, provides a very good description of how, why, and when medications help attention and memory.

There are several medical factors affecting attention, thus memory. Dr. E. M. Abrahamson and A. W. Pezet in their book, *Body, Mind and Sugar*, describe the symptoms, effect, and diagnostic procedures of the disorder known as hypoglycemia. Sugar, starches, and even protein, are converted into energy, or fuel, and stored in the liver. If there is too much sugar and the body cannot utilize it, we call the disorder diabetes; if there is too little sugar in the system, we do not have a sufficient fuel supply to call upon when needed. Hypoglycemia therefore results in fatigue, nervousness, possible trembling, apprehension, a feeling of sudden hunger, headaches, and mental restlessness and confusion.

Allergies can also create problems which interefere with school success. Ray C. Wunderlich, in *Allergy, Brains, and Children Coping,* describes symptoms and discusses treatment for children with behavior and academic problems related to brain dysfunction and allergy.

The child may be tested, and the psychologist recommends training in memory. A teacher asks, *"What* activities do I use?" In fact, this is the best question to ask provided we add to this question, *"Why* is his memory poor?"

MEMORY: RECEPTIVE STAGE

In the preceding chapters we have discussed the need for accurate intake of data. We question that if intake of stimuli, or the receptive stage, is not accurate, the image received is not consistent from one time to the next; thus, how can memory be accurate?

Our first step in the improvement of memory, therefore, becomes the improvement of any inefficiently operating receptive avenue. This may be done in a combination of therapy directed toward strengthening the weakness while, at the same time, data is fed to the student through his open or strong learning avenue. Each of the activities in the preceding chapters have tried to provide this combination. These activities take into consideration increasing attention (and memory) through active participation *during* the intake step, as opposed to intake by vision alone followed by a delayed response which is actually a test situation testing recall, rather than a learning experience. Following are further generalizations regarding improvement of input for recall. When intake accuracy is achieved, memory may no longer be seen as a problem.

Input should begin with the body. There is no substitute in learning for doing something yourself.

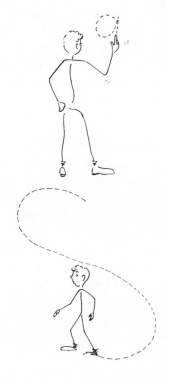

Have a student make a number or letter in the air with his arm. Have the class guess what it is.

Have the student move along the floor to form a number or letter and guess what it is.

The Kirshner Body Alphabet teaches the alphabet through imitation of form with the whole body.

Pantomine an action just demonstrated by the teacher. Have the class guess what it is.

When input is primarily through vision, an attention focuser during the observation period may be needed to direct focus to specific data. For example: "Go for a walk around the room or the yard. Take a model of what you will look for." The model may be a circle ("Find everything round"), a color ("Find everything red"), a pattern ("Find everything plaid"), a set of items ("Find all types of leaves"). Later a picture clue can be substituted.

If going to a fire house, give a picture clue card of all the items to look for: Pole, truck, beds, kitchen, etc.

Reproduction of what is viewed should immediately follow to insure accuracy of intake and to help fix a visual image.

Discussion helps by bringing into play the auditory/vocal input to stimulate visual imagery. At first, the child may need a picture clue shown to trigger memory of what was viewed. This is recognition memory and differs from producing a visual image without a stimulating visual clue.

Recognition memory is recall triggered by recognition of a previously introduced stimulus when it is repeated. Many people depend upon this level of recall. They will say, "Let me see it (or hear it) and I will tell you if it is correct." Being able to reproduce without any triggering stimulus is a higher level recall and requires being able to obtain a mental image.

Drawing (if appropriate skill) of floor plans working with the actual room or rooms reinforces placement and presence of things seen and boosts recall. Discuss and compare.

Building with toys (store, gas station, fire house pieces) lets a child reconstruct from memory the placement and absence or presence of things just seen. Discuss and compare and utilize recognition memory to make corrections.

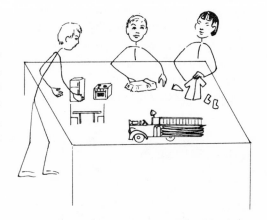

A teacher may present and demonstrate the finest lesson, but he has no way of knowing what the child is actually getting out of a lesson or an experience until he asks him to repeat the activity or to recognize the stimuli when presented again. At this point, if he does so incorrectly, the teacher tries to correct his response by presenting the stimuli to him again. However, each time he responds inaccurately, he is fixing an incorrect image in his mind and impressing an incorrect movement in his motor response circuits. Children with perceptual (and memory) deficiencies will find themselves thinking, "Which was the right way?" as conflicting images or responses are all stored; and he cannot recall which was the correct one.

Working to a model until the child no longer needs to do so is one way to insure only positive input and prevent trial-and-error work.

Puzzles can be invaluable in developing memory if done in the following manner. Place the puzzle pieces at one table and the frame at another. The child must look at the frame and decide what piece he will need ("one half of a plane, with the nose part"); he then goes to find this piece. He must keep the image in his mind while he travels the distance to the area containing the pieces and he must recognize the needed piece when he sees it. Thus, he "stretches" his visual memory. He must always work by meaningful clues, never by shape, color, or size alone. For further details and uses of puzzles, see Banas and Yelen's *Puzzle Power*.

The static visual *key cards* described throughout this book can also be placed a distance away from the student's work area. The student must, therefore, start his problem, physically go to the key card holding the visual image (mentally) of what is needed, recognize the answer, then hold the answer mentally while he returns to the work area and executes the answer. The distance can be increased until memory is achieved without needing to go and look at the key card (but the key should always be checked immediately upon finishing his work, so that the child, not the teacher, decides if the answer is correct).

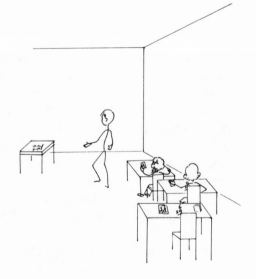

Viewing of partial models requires visualizing the missing section. Use of puzzles is the first step in learning to recognize missing parts. The student should show competency in working with meaningful puzzles before working with abstracts and symbols. Then partial letters, numbers, missing vowels from words, etc., can be presented. "Copy the form and add the missing part (s)." This taps recognition memory, but only partial clues are provided and reduced in amount to aid the child in developing visual images accurately and automatically.

Tracing, followed by eyes-closed reproduction, adds the motor avenue, intensifies concentration, and utilizes body imagery when copying or recalling with eyes open.

Tracking books can be a good mode of rapid recognition of a symbol or form, as the child must find the symbol from among many stimuli, rapidly and repeatedly. Provide a model to match with to insure consistently correct reinforcement.

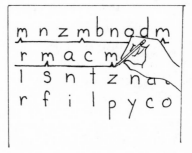

The game, Concentration, is very useful in developing immediate visual memory. Make sets of cards (3" x 5" file cards cut in half) containing ten pairs. The pairs can be anything from matching pictures to pictures, symbols to symbols, word with picture, math problems to answers, etc. Mix the cards and lay them out in a rectangular space, face down. As the child turns over a card, he must say what is on its face, then look for the appropriate matching card, turn it over, and say what is on it. If he finds a pair, he keeps it. Continue until all pairs are collected.

Homonyms, synonyms, and other easily confused reading, spelling, or math words can be best recalled through the associative method.

Discuss each word or symbol and its meaning. Print one to each half of an 8 1/2" x 11" sheet, folded to crease in the center. Add a picture clue under each. Add a phrase or sentence under each and fold the sheet so only one word at a time is seen. Trace three times. Have the children close their eyes and reproduce the word or problem on a scrap sheet. Share with the students the discovered differences in the pairs. File the words for review.

A sheet of 8 1/2" x 11" tagboard can be ruled into segments and word card strips cut to fit into each space the size of 3/4" x 2". As the child learns a new word, he prints it on the strip, places an illustrative picture on the back of the strip, then places the same picture clue on the tagboard. Following this, he can keep his words in an envelope

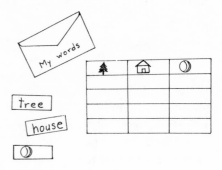

and at any time take them out and practice placing the words in the correct square on the tagboard. He can check himself by looking at the picture side of the word card for a match to the model.

Math number facts seem to be one of the really difficult memory problems. This is probably due to the lack of meaningfulness on which to hang recall as we can do with words. "Tricks" are a very useful way to trigger memory for a great many of our math needs. However, they *must* be illustrated on key cards, which will be used as a static visual referent until the trick is thoroughly learned. The trick is not to be the answer, but a clue to recall the answer.

A number line is the most basic visual aid which offers a clue to the answers for beginning addition and subtraction. Instead of rote im-printing, ± 1 and ± 2, the student is taught to visualize the figures on a number line. This will only work if the student can shift readily, as he will have to move forward visually for + 1 or + 2 when adding, and move backward (to the left) when subtracting. He should *not* count by ones, but learn to visualize the jump.

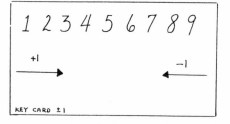

The "Teens Trick" can eliminate the need to memorize subtraction facts over ten. It is based on working with tens. "When subtracting 7 from 16 take the 7 away from 10 rather than from 16. The answer is 3. The 3 is then added to the ones-place number (6). This addition is the answer to the problem." To be sure, the child can subtract from 10 accurately the tens combinations which are placed at the side of the key card. This process, as illustrated, must be written onto a 3" x 5" card by the student and used as a reminder as he works.

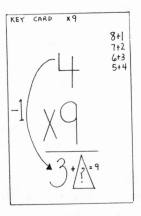

For multiplication facts there are several tricks.

When multiplying by 9, think one less than the number being multiplied by 9. Place that number under the problem to the left (or tens place). Now find the number which added to it will be 9. Place that number to the right of the first number (in the ones place). You now have your full answer. The combinations of nine should be on the key cards for accuracy in adding to nine.

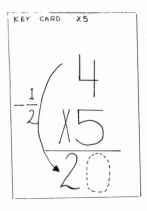

When multiplying by 5, think one half of the number being multiplied by 5. Place the answer under the problem to the left (tens place). Ask yourself, "Is there a remainder (does it divide in half evenly)?" If so, put a zero to the right of that number (ones place). That is your answer. If an uneven number, place a 5 (one half of base ten) next to your first number. That is your answer. Children should begin to visualize the odd (3,5,7,9) and even (2,4,6,8,) numbers and automatically place 0 or 5 appropriately in the answer. Don't forget to place these illustrations on individual key cards to be used by the students until no longer needed.

The terms used in math also present a memory problem for many children. This problem can also be solved with the use of key cards. The key to recall should be a meaningful cartoon type picture of the definition. Anything that will vividly portray the meaning of the term, such as illustrated here with proper and improper fractions, has been found to be a very successful memory boost.

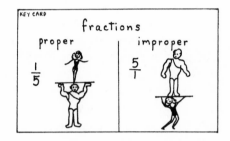

The steps (processes) required in solving math problems can cause a great deal of trouble for some students because they require shifting directionality, shifting from one process to another and back again (as in division, where one must divide, then multiply, then subtract, and start over again); they require good figure/ground perception, accurate spatial awareness, and accurate memory for number facts.

Drill alone, because it usually constitutes a trial-and-error approach, often fails to provide necessary long-range recall. Meaning and manipulation help a great deal to boost memory.

Introduce the concept of multiplication as repeated addition by illustrating with doubles (x2). Show that it means the same to say "4 two times" as it does to say 4 + 4."

Use a counting frame, buttons, or straws which the child can manipulate to illustrate the problem presented verbally, "Show me 4 two times."

Present the problem visually with flash cards (2 x 4) saying, "Show me the meaning of this problem by placing your buttons in proper combination."

Next, say "Show me two ways to write a problem that says 6 two times" (6 + 6 or 2 x 6). If the child cannot make the jump from manipulative objects to symbols, provide a number box as illustrated. It is essential that the number box contain slips that reinforce place value. Thus, the ones slips would be half the size of the tens, so they can be placed on a tens card and cover only the zero contained thereon.

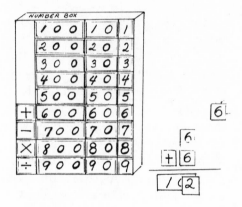

Have the child choose the correct symbol cards from the number box so that his choice of symbols shows his understanding the problem (2 x 6). Be sure he includes the addition sign from the number box.

Reinforce the meaning of multiplication (no answers are solicited at this step) by continuing to present oral and visual (symbol) problems of all kinds. The child illustrates his understanding of the problems presented by proper grouping of objects or symbols, as illustrated with 5 x 2 and 2 x 5.

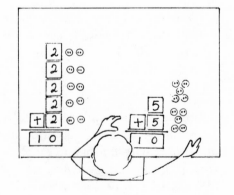

Now, introduce the concept of multiplication with zero and with ones. Go through the steps as outlined above and continue to the answer as part of this training step.

Introduce the concept of division by using straws or other similar manipulative devices. Show how to divide a group (even amounts) in half, and introduce the symbols ÷ 2 and 2⟌

Present problems verbally, ("Show me 6 divided in half"), and have the students manipulate the buttons at their desk to show their understanding of the concept.

Then, present visually, with a symbol problem (2⟌ 5 and 5 ÷ 2—show both ways), while children manipulate their buttons to show their understanding. No answer is necessary at this stage.

Have the children write the problems from verbal clues. "Show me how to write 5 divided by 2."

From the number box set up two each of the number cards through 10, as illustrated. Draw a line under each set. Add each set and place the proper number card under the line for each problem. Ask the children, "What is half of the sum?" They should be able to point to either card of the set (above the line) to show understanding of the concept of dividing into two equal parts from symbols. This should lead to the concept of division as the inverse process of multiplication. Always present the problem symbolically as well as manipulatively.

1	2	3	4	5	6	7	8	9	10
1	2	3	4	5	6	7	8	9	10
2	4	6	8	10	12	14	16	18	20

Provide a set of Cuisenaire Rods® or Mills Center Blocks® to each child,* or make a set of number value strips on cardboard that follow the same concept of providing proper size relationships (see illustration).

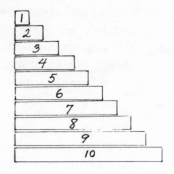

Each child should have a set containing twelve 1's, three 2's, four 3's, three 4's, three 5's, two 6's, two 7's, two 8's, two 9's, and one 10.

Place three, four, or more of the number one ☐ blocks or strips on the desk in left-to-right fashion, as a train. "If these were added together what would be the sum? Find one strip large enough to cover the train and place it below the individual ones number cards. Can you find any other repeated numbers that will make this total?" Now reverse the problem. "How many 1's (3's, 2's) could be taken out of 6?" Or, "How many times can 6 be divided by 1 (3, or 2)?" Repeat this procedure over and over again with different numbers until the words *divided by* take on meaning.

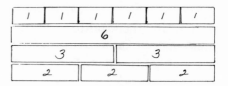

$$6 \div 2 =$$

Another approach is to have the student take any number, write it, and subtract the presented divisor until he comes to zero. He then counts how many times he took that number away by counting the number of subtraction signs.

$$
\begin{array}{r}
6 \\
-2 \\
\hline
4 \quad \text{1.} \\
-2 \\
\hline
2 \quad \text{2.} \\
-2 \\
\hline
0 \quad \text{3.}
\end{array}
$$

*Cuisenaire Rods have been developed by the Cuisenaire Company of America, Inc., 12 Church St., Rochelle, New York; and Mills Center Blocks have been developed by the Mills Center of Ft. Lauderdale, Florida.

Set up arrays, introducing the concept of the "missing number" from a multiplication problem. This will reinforce division as the inverse process of multiplication, introduce checking, and establish a visual concept clue for learning division facts.

$$6 \div \boxed{?} = 3 \times \begin{array}{|c|c|c|} \hline ? & ? & ? \\ \hline ? & ? & ? \\ \hline \end{array}$$

$$\boxed{?} \times 3 = 6 \qquad \boxed{?}\boxed{?}\boxed{?} = 6$$

Each division key card would be a multiplication reminder.

$$
\begin{array}{rl}
3x & \\
? & = 3 \\
 & = 6 \\
 & = 9 \\
 & = 12 \\
 & = 15 \\
 & = 18 \\
 & = 21 \\
 & = 24 \\
 & = 27 \\
\end{array}
$$

KEY CARD   ÷3

MEMORY: EXPRESSIVE STAGE

When we ask a child to respond (show he remembers what he has been taught), he has to use a portion of his body through which to express his response. We are now looking at the end product of a complicated journey.

We are not looking into his brain and cannot see into his storage compartments to know if data is present or is in a place from which it can be quickly retrieved. We are not even looking at the message-carrying circuits of his nervous system to see if all the junctions and pathways are available to carry messages into and away from the brain.

If the child is to use vision, (recognize a word on a page), do we know that his visual apparatus (eyes and neurological connections to the brain) is responding adequately? If he is to use a motor response (as when writing his answer), do we know that the musculature he needs to bring into play is adequately developed, so that he can illustrate what he means to show us? Or that visual/motor coordination allows his hand to reproduce what his eye sees?

If the answer to any of these questions is negative, training would be given to increase efficiency of the expressive avenues before we can say that memory of the data taught is missing.

Ask him to respond with a different pathway. For example, many severe learning disability students cannot read or write adequately, yet can attend college where they learn and are tested auditorily. Many children practice their spelling test at home only to fail it in school. Upon questioning, they revealed they practiced (and can spell) orally, but could not take a written test. Analysis shows that they know verbally which symbols to use, but could not remember (visually) quickly enough how to form the symbol. Many learning disability children (and adults) have been known to say, "I have it up here (pointing to the head), but can't get it down there (pointing to arm and hand)."

MEMORY: NEUROLOGICAL ORGANIZATION

If both receptive and expressive avenues appear to be functioning well, and motivation and attention are good, the neurological organization of the student needs to be investigated to find out if the storage and retrieval centers are doing their job. There are many conflicts among professionals as to how this system can be measured and what influences the system.

One of the most useful approaches is the administration of a natural sleep electroencephalograph (EEG). The patterns which are obtained from this brain wave testing reveal intensity, depression, and/or interruptions in the electrical rhythms of the brain. These rhythms are felt to be indicative of stages of awareness and unawareness to stimuli and would have a direct bearing on memory. The location of any dysrhythmias suggests the learning mode which will be deficient and tells us avenues to avoid when presenting data to be learned. For example, if in the area of the brain controlling reception of visual clues, we would switch to motor or oral input.

It is often reported that the EEG pattern is immature, and the child will, therefore, outgrow his learning problem. This may well be true, but as long as we present tasks to his immature system that it is not ready to handle, the student may fail to learn and/or learning will be difficult.

Another EEG pattern can reveal the presence of petit mal seizure activity, though the pupil has never shown outward (obvious) signs of seizures. With petit mal seizure activity, he may be noted to "stare into space" at times and to require a touch to bring his attention back to the task.

The seizure episode is unknown to the child who momentarily loses contact, possibly many times a day. During these losses of contact he will lose the thread of the lesson, fail to store just previously received stimuli, and we see him as forgetful, inattentive, and having very fluctuating memory. Medication can control seizure activity and may markedly increase school performance.

Another approach to identification and remediation of the storage and retrieval centers is held by the Institutes for the Achievement of Human Potential in Philadelphia and developed by Dr. Glenn Doman and Dr. Charles Delacato. Their theory involves the premise that man is the only animal that has reached the stage of development where the brain is divided into two distinct halves, one of which becomes dominant over the other and becomes the one that controls skills. A lack of the development of this hemispheric dominance, they believe, would reflect in an inability to handle the code of our language.

Thus, dominance, expressed in choice of handedness, footedness, and eyedness, reflects the presence or lack of hemispheric dominance. From this theory has come a revolutionary and controversial therapeutic program now adapted for use by parent and teacher and clearly outlined in Delacato's *A New Start for Children with Reading Problems.* Literature and personal experience have shown that one of the few consistent symptoms when a learning and memory problem is present is the lack of hemispheric dominance. It may be reflected in ambilateral use of limbs or in a mixed dominance, where one hand is favored, but the opposite eye is preferred. Research is showing a relationship between these two types of lack of dominance and specific learning problems. The ambilateral child is seen most often as making visual perceptual errors and having poor body awareness, while the mixed dominance is associated with the language disability, where word retrieval is deficient, or language and its referent are confused. (see Banas and Wills, *Success Begins with Understanding.)*

VISUAL MEMORY: ATTENTION AND CONCENTRATION

Many children remain a puzzle because they can do an activity correctly one minute and not the next. They are the children with so-called careless errors; and, indeed, they can correct their errors if the teacher focuses their attention to them. An EEG shows no abnormality nor immaturity.

The fluctuation in performance is maddening, and efforts to pay attention are inconsistent. This is true for both children taking and children not taking medication as an attention aid. These children do try to pay attention; but they cannot seem to focus their attention consistently at the optimum place nor maintain their focus. Thus, they may be paying attention, but they are not able to concentrate attention accurately enough or long enough to fix a correct and consistent image.

Methods should be used that slow the viewing pace. Try underlining, tracing, and manipulative materials. These aid concentration by increasing time of fixation on the stimuli.

Try intensifying the elements with color, tactile experiences, large type, a lot of open space around problems or between lines, or even single problems to a page. These approaches should be used to help focus attention on key elements and reduce intensity and interference from surrounding stimuli.

Exercises can be used to improve visual tracking and fixating. This should be provided by visual specialists and can help develop better concentration; often reading and math efficiency jumps significantly afterward.

Bring into play another area of the brain. Verbalizing (softly, but aloud) has been found to significantly decrease visual perceptual errors. Have the student talk his way through a problem and watch accuracy increase.

Chapter 8

Learning to listen

OVER half the child's day is spent responding to the auditory aspect of his environment. He gains a great deal of information from auditory clues. He hears a sound and rushes out to greet the ice cream man. He listens to the news broadcast on the radio and hears that a hurricane is near, and rushes out to tell his friends that school may be closed tomorrow. He also has to retain what he hears, as when Mother tells him to go to the store, and he tries to recall what items she wanted him to get.

He must take in, hold, interpret, and be able to reproduce sounds accurately. Words are but groups of sounds in a specific sequence, and sentences are words strung together in a series. Any change of placement alters the meaning derived from these sounds.

Listening involves attention span, discrimination of the likeness and difference between sounds or words, directional and sequential organization of sounds and words, and perception of the meaning of sounds and words.

The first step in learning to respond to the auditory environment is to stop and listen to it. Learning to listen involves the development of attention and increasing its span, and learning what to listen for from among the multitude of sounds that bombard our ears all day.

ATTENDING

Listening requires the ability to attend to sounds and to language. Start with games and activities which teach the child to increase attention span, to listen for specific stimuli, and to take turns.

Jack-in-the-box

Have the children crouch down and listen as you sing, "Pop Goes the Weasel." When they hear "pop" they are to jump high into the air.

140

Circle Games

1. Have the children sit in a circle and assign a number to each one. Have one player stand inside the circle. This player calls a number. The child with that number runs into the circle and executes an action, such as catching a ball, tagging, etc. The action is established initially and remains the same throughout the game, so the child has to listen for his number only.

Players in circle games can be numbered consecutively (1,2,3,1,2, etc.). Teacher calls out, "All the 1's run (or jump in place or stand)." Now the children must listen for their number and for what they are to do when they hear it.

Words can be substituted for numbers so that the listening and perception increases in complexity. Duck, Duck, Goose is a common game in which the children sit in a circle. One child moves about the outside of the circle tapping each child in turn as he says "duck, duck," then suddenly says "goose!" The "goose" must run out of the circle and try to catch the tapper before the tapper runs around the circle and takes the empty space. In this way the attention span is lengthened.

Songs

Songs such as "One Finger, One Thumb, One Hand, Keep Moving" are excellent for reinforcing identification of body parts, as well as listening. Keep adding a part of the body until all parts are mentioned. Demonstrate as you sing.

Have children line up, arms a short distance apart, facing the teacher (one or two lines deep). Teacher calls out in slow rhythm (increasing speed of calls each lesson), "Touch your . . . toes, hips, eyes, lips, etc." Show as you speak, so a child can correct it if he interprets incorrectly at first.

Then use the Simon Says game so that the children do not get tired of the exercise too easily.

Story Telling

5₁

The Teacher relates or reads an imaginary story to the children, and the children are asked to act out the parts of the story. The story might go as follows:

Johnny was *walking* to school and he met his friend, Billy. He stopped to talk to Billy. Billy told him that he had learned to *hop.* First he *hopped on his right foot,* then he *hopped on his left foot.* Johnny tried to *hop on his right foot.* Johnny tried to *hop on his left foot.* Johnny's feet got all mixed up. Johnny *fell down to the floor.* Johnny *picked himself up* and started to *skip.* He heard the bell at the school and *ran* to get there on time.

Variations of types of stories and types of activities in stories may be used.

Taking A Walk

Children need opportunities to organize the auditory aspect of their environment. Take them for a walk and (a) locate the source of sounds, (b) find low sounds, loud sounds, etc., (c) identify common sounds (a bell, a horn, etc.), (d) imitate sounds (where applicable).

Prepare ahead to listen for specific sounds. Give children a visual clue (picture of what they are to listen for) to take with them on the walk as an aid to concentration on what to listen for.

In the Classroom

"Raise your hand when you hear . . . (call off a series of words)." Have the students raise their hands when they hear a word or sound repeated when a list is read. Next have only a specified child respond. Say, "John, tell me when you hear . . ."

Next, have the children repeat the word when heard to insure accuracy. "As I read this story, each time I say . . .you repeat it." Build to two words or more to be listened for. Work with eyes closed.

The same type of training as that above in all steps can be done with nonsense words, sentences or phrases.

Pass It On

In a low, well-modulated voice, say a sentence to a child close to his ear. Have him repeat the sentence out loud. Begin in front of the pupil who has his eyes closed. Later speak from his side, then from behind him.

Have a child tell another child a sentence in a low voice, but not a whisper tone. Have each child in turn repeat this sentence to the next child until the last pupil stands and says it out loud for verification with the original.

AUDITORY DISCRIMINATION

Background, habit, inattention, or disability may influence how a child hears and interprets sounds. In a common example, the child may hear *pin* and think he heard *pen*. In a more complex situation the misinterpretation may cause incorrect learning of new words and names, poor spelling, and inaccurate following of directions. When children learn by rote, misinterpretations can become a major problem as content clue or common sense is not available to correct errors of intake.

Auditory adequacy can be checked by an audiometer, an instrument which measures auditory acuity or the recognition of the discrete units of sound. The ability to interpret what is heard requires more than awareness of the presence of a sound; it requires very accurate discrimination or differentiation between sounds and retention of what is heard in a specific sequence.

The child who does not get instructions given orally may be frequently called inattentive or hard-of-hearing. The audiometric evaluation reveals normal levels of acuity, yet errors from inaccurate discrimination of speech sounds are obviously present in his responses. Frequent ear infections, asthma, or swollen adenoids at the very early years when the child first learned sounds could have affected the intake, thus interpretation and recall of sounds.

Though later hearing may be normal, habits from early learning experiences remain fixed.

Children have varying degrees of ability in auditory discrimination, and the maturation of the skill is gradual and is often not fully developed before the age of eight. Poor auditory discrimination is related to poor achievement in reading and spelling in which instruction begins from the age of four or five upward, ready or not.

The teaching of a phonetic system (sound and its symbol referent) is an important part of any reading or spelling program. The child who does not know the sound/symbol code of his language cannot read beyond his capacity to memorize and to retain a sight vocabulary.

When words become similar in configuration (shape) and in structure (sequence of letters), the child may find it increasingly difficult to learn through a sight method. If he cannot hear the differences between sounds that are similar, he will likewise have difficulty learning and using the phonetic code. The spelling errors of children with poor auditory discrimination will reveal characteristic errors involving substitution of similar sounds, especially the following:

short	e/i	(pen/pin)
short	o/u	(pot/put)
short	e/a	(met/mat)
	b/p	(Ben/pen)
	t/d	(Ted/dead)
	f/v	(fan/van)
	s/z	(Sue/zoo)
	sh/ch	(shoe/chew)
	br/bir	(ur,er) (brush/birch)

Looking at one fifth grader's spelling test paper, we will see all the characteristic auditory errors.

Oct. 1, 1975

	Student spelling	Correct word
1	adop	adopt
2	arplane	airplane
3	alfbet	alphabet
4	amouge	among
5	aMout	amount
6	apreashate	appreciate
7	apreashathion	appreciation
8	arifmtic	arithmetic
9	armys	armies
10	arow	arrow
11	aret	art
12	aretist	artist
13	atak	attack
14	babys	babies
15	batls	battles
16	buaty	beauty
17	bares	berries
18	birth	birth
19	blaket	blanket
20	bluod	blood

Establish that the child's speech patterns are adequate or he will not reinforce sounds (to himself) accurately. If speech is poor, first check tongue mobility. The child should be able to move his tongue freely upward, toward the nose and out of the mouth, over the lips to the left and to the right. It is also important to have free movement of the mouth (lips) to be able to form the appropriate sounds.

If he cannot do so, training must be given until tongue movement is adequate for the job it must do in forming speech sounds. This would precede all other forms of speech work.

If he does not use (but *can* produce) good speech habits, utilize appropriate speech techniques for establishing oral speech patterns. Associate sounds with words and pictures at the same time, while building a speech notebook.

An alphabet box should be built out of shoe boxes or a tool case. Each of its drawers should contain a variety of concrete representatives for the sounds of the consonant and the short vowel symbols. In the *t* drawer, for example, is possibly a toy table, miniature telephone, tiger, etc. These objects, as opposed to the usual method of collecting pictures, can be handled kinesthetically and the children more easily relate to them. Note that the object must be associated *in the same lesson* with the symbol, thus each

box has on its face a picture and the symbol. The association should be as meaningful as possible.

Appropriate associative word pictures are a key to accurate intake, thus accurate recall. Pictures (or words) that do not illustrate the sound in question clearly or isolated enough will not clarify or intensify sound input and may confuse it. For example, the picture and word—*octopus*—are often used as the clue to the short ŏ sound. It is not only too long a word, but it contains the symbol *o* twice, where *o* has two different sounds. A far better association is illustrated and is explained by saying, "When you go to the dentist he asks you to open your mouth wide *o* and you are to say "ah."

Select two or three symbols with widely differing sounds and shapes (do not use *h* and *n* in the same lesson at first, nor *m, n,* for example). Remove the drawers or boxes containing the objects representing the chosen sounds. Place them on the table before the group. Take out one item at a time and listen for the initial sound. Mix the objects from all three boxes.

Provide a key card on which the letter and the sound clue picture is written for each of the sounds in the lesson. In turn, have a child pick up any object, say it, listen for its initial sound, and place it on the sheet to which it belongs (or sort directly to the boxes).

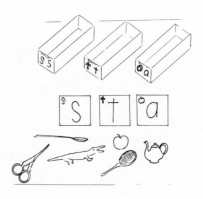

Introduce symbols regularly, and change as needed for reinforcement.

Do not teach two sounds at the same time which are easily confused. For example, if the child has trouble with short i and short e, do not drill him on both to get at the difference. Rather, take one sound and teach it thoroughly. Then teach the other sound and teach it thoroughly. At this point mix the sounds by practicing sorting between them.

The alphabet boxes should not be extended to provide a drawer for each of the digraphs — *ch, sh, th, wh* — as these sounds may be troublesome for children with a lag in auditory discrimination. Use as instructed above.

Another set of boxes will be needed for those with poor auditory discrimination. These should contain blends, as illustrated. Practice should be with the appropriate symbols represented as a *single unit*. Use as instructed above.

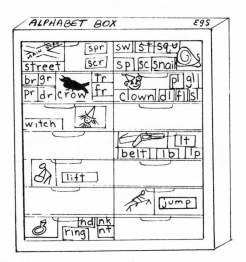

Chapter 9

Auditory perceptual constancy

A CHILD learns language by imitation and reinforcement. At first he may associate only identically reproduced sounds as being the same. Soon, however, he recognizes that although there may be some change of sound within a sound group (word), the meaning of the sound group is constant because it always is associated with the same object or action. If a word said by someone from the eastern shores of New England was to be compared with the same word said by someone from the Deep South or with the twang of the midwesterner, some of the sounds within the word would be different, but the sound group as a whole would have the same meaning. This meaning and the differences in phonetic reproduction are accepted because the context remains the same.

A step in auditory constancy is made when the child recognizes the word *mother* as the same as *mom,* or *mummy*. Again the referent is constant, though the sound (language) unit varies.

Further factors which affect perceptual constancy in communication are language cadences and rhythms. Raising the voice at the end of a sentence usually indicates (in English) asking a question. But there are countries in which the end of the sentence is usually raised and does not constitute a question. The lack of constancy in sounds and patterns from one language to another may be one reason why some people cannot seem to be able to learn to listen in another language, even though they have learned to read in it. To train the student in recognizing sound units as having the same meaning, use a static visual clue to develop an accurate auditory/visual match.

Auditory closure is also involved in perceptual constancy. It refers to a process of filling in for unheard, distorted, or unfamiliar sound elements in a meaningful word by using past experience or familiarity of the rest of the sound pattern. For example, without auditory closure communication would be difficult, since outside sounds, the poor enunciation of other sounds and fluctuating attention may cause the child to miss some sounds or words.

Whenever unusual pronunciations or dialects change the sound patterns, lack of concentration causes one to hear only partially what was spoken; or a word or sentence is spoken a different way than he expected to hear it. Some children cannot use blending because c ă t remains ku ă tu, rather than becoming *cat*. The lack of closure ability would require that the student be taught the whole word by a sight method, rather than through a phonics approach, until therapy can improve the auditory avenue.

David F. Barr has written an excellent text, *Auditory Perceptual Disorders*, on assessment of auditory perceptual problems. His definition and diagnostic guidelines will be valuable in understanding the importance of auditory therapy in school success.

If the child has a specific hearing deficiency or lag which affects reception of certain sounds, he may need some lipreading training to pick up these missed sounds visually as he listens. His experiential background can help auditory perception by interpreting from minimal clues from the meaning of the context, but a visual referent presented as he listens will assure accurate interpretation.

Bingo can be used for reinforcement of the automatic reaction to a symbol and its sound and the development of accurate listening skills.

Instruct pupils to fold a sheet of 8 1/2" x 11" paper in half and in half again. Open the sheet and fold in half and in half again the other way. Then open, and the folds will provide sixteen Bingo boxes per sheet. Encase in a plastic protector and use with a grease crayon that can be rubbed off after each lesson.

Take the lesson to be reinforced and (1) distribute pictures or (2) print a letter or (3) word on the board. Instruct the students to place a picture or copy a word in any box on their paper. (Have random placement so Bingo cards differ when completed.) Do box by box until all boxes are filled with a different picture or symbol. Add the appropriate picture clue wherever needed with the symbols to assure a positive learning response during this game. Keep a sheet for the master card. (Check cards to be sure copied word or symbol is correct.) Place the Bingo cards in a plastic protector.

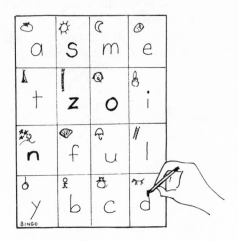

Pass grease crayon to be used to trace the stimulus called until one line across, down, or horizontally is completed as in Bingo.

Play by calling out a symbol, sound, word, or an instruction regarding a word until someone gets Bingo, and then begin again.

Rub off marks and save the cards to play on other days. Use for about a week and make new ones for each lesson as suggested in the following ways.

Discrimination Use picture cards. Say a sound. Have the class indicate which picture begins with this sound and write the correct symbol on the picture. Continue until Bingo is won. Repeat, but the sound may be found in final or median position.

Auditory/Visual Match. Use a letter card. Say a sound; have the students trace the proper letter(s) representing the sound.

Closure or Constancy.
Which word rhymes with ＿＿＿＿＿ ?
Which word has a long *a* ?
Which word has *ow* saying "ouch?"

Word lists can be made from the readers to use in auditory discrimination and closure activities. They may also be used for spelling lesson reinforcement. No matter what the purpose of the word list, it must be kept in mind that the child must use all of his learning avenues (visual/auditory/kinesthetic/associative).

Provide paired words from which the child must choose one. Start with totally different pairs, then make initial changes, then change the endings, then the sequence, then change internal symbols to expand attention and ability. Say the words, enunciating very clearly. Have the children trace the letters of the word they hear — do not let them cross letters out. The pupils should add an associative picture to insure accurate auditory/visual match.

jump Ted	pat mat	pat pam
pat pot	was saw	sat scat
carpet car wet	freeze sneeze	this kiss

In establishing sound/symbol associations, the key is to preserve the constancy of the auditory, the visual, and the motor response; seeing an *m* is reinforced by saying "m" as the hand writes or the finger traces *m* while viewing a picture clue that shows the meaning of the symbol *m*.

This multisensory process combines the auditory/visual approach most commonly employed in teaching with kinesthetic/associative enrichment.

Following are examples of typical workbook exercises and suggestions for changing the instructions so that more accurate associations are made.

Suitable key cards should be provided to refer to when working or the exercise is a trial-and-error experience.

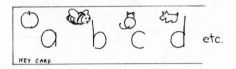

Note how the tracing of the symbol adds a kinesthetic reinforcement to heighten the visual recognition.

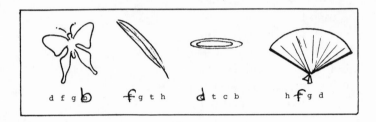

Recognition here is reinforced by copying, thus adding extra kinesthetic reinforcement. Note the whole work approach is important.

The rhyming elements should be kinesthetically chosen, thus combining sight recognition with tracing. A new meaningful total (for the picture) is created to reinforce blending knowledge.

Again, the tracing of like elements reinforces the visual discrimination of rhyming elements.

These words may be recopied in a list and an associative picture added next to each one to insure the child reads the total word meaningfully.

Blends should be placed as part of the whole word.

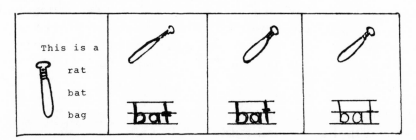

Completion and fill-in type *must* be combined with picture clue and tracing of the whole word. An initial model for matching is essential to avoid trial and error.

Chapter 10

Auditory sequencing and blending

D IRECTIONAL errors in auditory intake or memory may cause trouble with blending; c·a·t may become *tack.* For the child with reversal problems, words such as was/saw or no/on become a problem unless strong left/right approaches in visual and *auditory* sequencing are taught and reinforced.

In order to use the sound/symbol code of our language, the child must be able to blend units into new wholes. Blending ability may be deficient because of poor auditory memory, discrimination, closure, or sequencing, and may be the cause of inability to use phonics as a word attack skill.

Sound patterns as represented by symbols must be recognized visually. The English language is a complex one of symbol sequences which affect the sound to be produced. For example, note how the sound associated with *a* changes as a different symbol is placed next to it: *pat, par, Paul, pail, pare.*

Learning rules and being able to apply them is an almost impossible task without strong associative building blocks on which to draw from recall to application. It is for this reason that associative methods must be employed in teaching strong visual responses to sequence patterns, and that reinforcement must carry a child through more and more complex use of a skill in broadening application.

For children learning or having difficulty with the sequential nature of blending, begin with the alphabet box containing the objects representing the consonants and short vowel sounds. Take out two drawers containing sounds very different and easy to hear and to pronounce, and the short *a* drawer.

156

Show an object from the *ă* box. Say its sound. Choose an object from one of the consonant boxes and have the children say its initial sound. Slide these objects together (vowel first) as the children blend the sounds to produce a word *(at)*. Find an object from the other consonant box and say it as it slides in front of the two-sound word *sat.* Continue with a variety of combinations until the child can blend accurately.

A letter tray containing cards on which are printed the symbol and a picture clue are then used in the same way as above. A cookie sheet purchased in the food store can be painted with chalkboard paint. Cardboard letter sets made as illustrated can be backed with small squares cut from magnetic strips purchased at stationary stores. Thus, the letter set cannot fall off the tray, even if it becomes turned upside down. The letter cards should always be placed at the top of the tray in *abc* order. Consonants should be printed in black and vowels in red. After a child builds his word, he can copy it with chalk on the tray for additional reinforcement.

After the children practice enunciating the word with the teacher, hold up a picture of a simple three-letter word (cat). Have the children build the word by choosing the correct letter cards. At this stage they have to say the word to themselves (softly but aloud) and

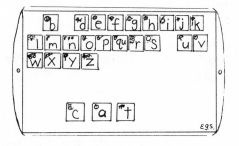

must learn to properly enunciate or
they will give themselves the wrong
sound clues. Spelling requires pro-
duction of the sound clues *from
within the individual,* from outside,
as when the teacher gives a spelling
test.

Blending practice, when extended to the linear level, may need
to be connected associatively with
the pictorial representation (as in
rebus reading).

A picture should be added after
the word is built to insure the child
reads it accurately. Some children
can spell words because they know
the symbol (visual association) to
use for sounds heard, yet cannot
read back the word just written
because they cannot produce the
sound for the visual.

By building a difficult word first with three-dimensional objects and then
manipulative symbols, the child sees the elements clearly and is less likely to
add or omit sounds (symbols). His blending will also hinge on directional
constancy as he draws the letters together in proper sequence. An arrow
should be placed at the top left-hand side of his work area until no longer
needed.

The alphabet box containing the
sounds of the blends must now be
used. Letter cards containing the
consonant symbols and a picture
clue should be included in each box
for building the blends in that box.
Blends may cause a problem because of poor auditory discrimination or difficulty with sequencing.

Begin with exercises in discriminating among sounds (as in the third activity under "Auditory Discrimination" in Chapter Eight) within one box of objects, then among the other boxes.

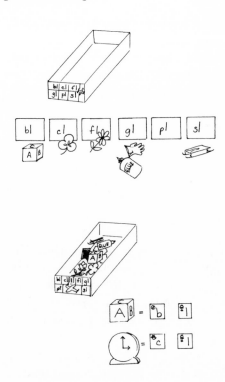

Match letter cards to the objects within a box. See how several symbols may be needed (and in what sequence) to represent each sound.

Next, place objects in proper sequence to show the child hears the sound units and their sequence in a word given to him to spell (give the word orally or by a picture). After checking correct sequencing of the objects, have the students write the letter representation below each (the several symbols representing a blend are written together).

The alphabet box set should be continued to the next level of phonetic difficulty, long vowel sounds. These are easy to hear but can be very difficult for children because of the fact that the sound/symbol association is less constant and the sequencing of the symbols that represent the single sound must be exact.

Long *a* sound may be spelled *mail, mate, may;*
long *e* sound: *meat, meet, mete, Jimmy;*
long *i* sound: *pie, pipe, sky, night;*
long *o* sound: *moat, mote, mow, old.*

The long *u* sound should be omitted at this time, as this sound has even greater numbers of symbol representations. Include vowel letter cards in each box as needed to represent the sound of that box. This reinforces the knowledge that only a limited number of symbols would be possible to represent each sound.

Provide a set of vowel associative key cards as illustrated, and teach a lesson which contains the following story.

* * * * *

Some vowels when together are like noisy children in line. The one behind can poke his friend in front and make him call out loudly (he says his name). But the friend behind says *nothing* and keeps out of trouble. If the teacher separates the noisy boys (vowels) by another child (a consonant), only *E* is big enough and can still reach over and poke his friend in front. But, if two children separate *E* from his friend, everyone talks quietly again (uses short sound).

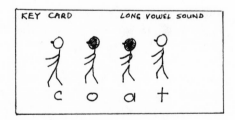

The friends that get into trouble are:

ai   ay

oa

ee   ee   ey

ie

and that big boy *E,* who causes trouble from the end of the line.

* * * * *

The same idea applies to the children in line where a vowel in front is quiet but at the end is noisy. Practice building words using the objects from the alphabet boxes and attaching with each object its appropriate letter card.

Provide a set of short vowel words on 3″ x 5″ file cards which are written as illustrated to provide space to insert a vowel letter card which will change the word to a long-vowel word. Provide a letter set of vowels. Say the word on the card, "mat," place an ☐e☐ card in the space provided. "What does it say now?" At first, use only final *e* changes; then introduce cards with internal changes.

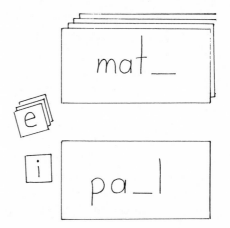

Shuffle each time for reinforcement and practice. Children can work independently after being sure they have the concept by writing the short-vowel word, then the long-vowel word, and putting a picture next to each to show they read them correctly.

Provide a set of single syllable words, some containing short vowels and some long vowels, one each to a 3″ x 5″ card. Print consonants in black and vowels in red. The children should shuffle the cards, then sort them to the rule key card. They should say the word, shuffle the cards and sort them. Afterwards the children copy the list and draw a picture to illustrate each word.

The Alpha-Omega Card Box, devised by the authors, is a supplement to the alphabet boxes.

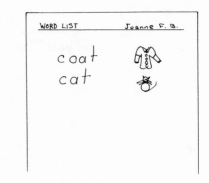

Have the words as presented, one each to a 3″ x 5″ file card of the color designated. The student then adds a picture to the back of each word card. The picture should clearly illustrate the word. Provide a file box with *abc* dividers whose tabs are reversed, so the sound/symbol pattern can be written on the tab. Add a picture clue to the sound of that section on the face of the file divider, as illustrated. Build a file with each section in the same order as in the alphabet boxes.

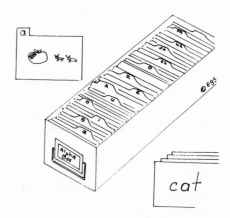

Use white 3″ x 5″ cards for the short vowel and digraph section; green cards for words with long vowel words and blends; pink cards for words with diphthongs; and yellow for advanced endings, such as *-ance, -tion*, etc.

The words in each section must be single syllable only. Words in the white section should be single syllable that have vowels that *only* produce a short vowel sound.

Incorrect	Correct
app̶l̶e̶	cap
c̶a̶rpet	pet

Words in the green section should be single syllable with vowels that produce only a long vowel sound.

Words in the pink section, likewise, are to be single syllable, but the vowels will be used in all the combinations called diphthongs.

Children should work from the picture side for auditory and spelling reinforcement. "Say the word, write it, check the word side for accuracy." Shuffle the word cards each time so order of presentation differs.

Have the children sort the cards and work with one sound/symbol unit (such as short *a*). Then take a second symbol which may be a long *a* or short *e* until it is learned. Shuffle the two card sets together and work with the two combined. Learn a third symbol and combine it with the first two. Continue to another, but drop one of the first three. This mixed practice will not combine more than three different sound/symbol units.

Always have key cards out for reference in order to stop trial-and-error work and to assure positive reinforcement. *Do not allow trial-and-error activity.*

Work from the word side to review sight recognition, phonetic attack, and/or meaning vocabulary. The children should decode the word and turn the card to the picture side to check their response.

Using a notebook or steno pad, the children head each page with a picture clue to each sound newly presented, and list words as learned down the left-hand side of the page. They then add a picture showing each word's meaning on the right-hand side. Then copy words into the book on the proper page by sound/symbol pattern, as a new word presents itself. This brings forth the involvement of the children in (a) finding the correct pattern page, (b) copying, (c) adding a meaningful picture, and (d) continuing visual and auditory reinforcement.

An alternate activity would be to have the pupils go to their reader or workbook and find all the words or a specific number of words that fit a certain pattern and list them on the proper page.

For homework they add the word picture to illustrate the meaning and to show they could read the words.

To develop sound/symbol accuracy with multisyllable words, an associative/manipulative approach is still needed to aid the ability to break the whole into manageable auditory units. The sound units can be most readily learned if the child can *see* the elements as he listens for the parts.

Print small words on 1″ x 3″ strips. Place words in two columns, but in random order to be combined in game or puzzle fashion. "Find the words that put together say *carpet,* or "Find a word that tells what covers the floor." (carpet) Be certain that all parts are familiar in isolation, for example: *car* and *pet.* The children should

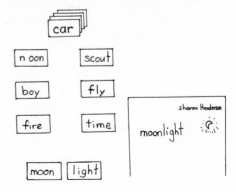

place the combined words on a list and illustrate new words.

Children can compete against a clock until they find all the words they can. They then copy the newly built words and add their associative pictures which are needed to assure they built and read the words correctly. A picture should be drawn for the new word only. Otherwise, conceptual confusion might arise for the meaning.

Words can be built with the same principle above using common endings or prefixes and suffixes. (Do not use short vowel words at first, so that the need to double the final consonant does not arise.) Always list, then illustrate.

Children may like to challenge each other by writing compound words, then cutting them apart for another student to rematch.

Place a set of multisyllable words at the end of each section in the alphabet card box (using proper color 3″ x 5″ cards). *Be sure that no sound unit is included that has not already been introduced.*

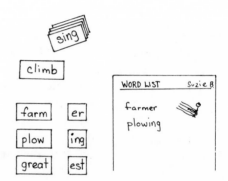

Short Vowel Section
(white)

Incorrect	*Correct*
fireman	radish
+ long	
market	packet
+ diphthong	short only

Long Vowel Section
(green)

Incorrect	*Correct*

paper
  + diphthong
	mailman
	  long & short

nation
  + suffix
	waste basket
	  long & short
	  & blend

Use the word cards as instructed: the picture side for auditory to symbol recall, the word side for symbol to auditory recall.

Syllabification by phonics rules is more difficult and more advanced. Until the children know all the spelling/vowel patterns, provide key cards as illustrated. Put a word that is unknown to the children on the board. Have the pupils try to guess the word by dividing it in all possible fashions, seeing how the sounds would differ with placement. Try various ways until the word sounds familiar.

Rules regarding sequencing of symbols may not result in transfer nor allow flexible application because, perceptually, the child did not really understand what was meant and learned the rule by rote only. What he can do on an end-of-the-week test or in a structured workbook page does not seem at all related to word attack skills when he needs to apply them in reading or spelling.

The need for strong associations and the need to use these associative keys during the reinforcement period, as well as during the initial learning period, is of the utmost importance.

Dramatic illustrations in story and pictorial form can be vastly effective in improving recall for phonics rules as well as rules and concepts in math, English grammar, syntax, and punctuation.

For example, for the rule regarding *c* followed by *e i y,* a story can be developed by the teacher as the children watch:*

* * * * *

Here is a cat who is very annoyed because he is being followed by his pesty baby brothers. When a cat is annoyed, what does he say? He says, "SSSSSsssss." Do you know the names of his pesty followers? Yes, *e i y.* (Fill in those letters only when reaching that part of the story.)

* * * * *

Following the preceding demonstration, have the child make his own associative key card with this illustration. When he makes his own key, the kinesthetic activity helps to focus his attention on all the details and shows the teacher whether he has attended accurately.

Provide a list of words which help the child discriminate in the use of this new concept. Instruct him, "Find all the pests in the following list of words and draw the cat over them. Remember, they are only a pest if they are following *c.*" The child should refer to a key card as he works.

---

*This story and illustration are reprinted from Norma Banas's and I. H. Wills's book, *Success Begins With Understanding,* p. 39, with the permission of Academic Therapy Publications.

Next, the child should head a paper with a happy cat and an angry cat, putting all the words with the *happy* cat *(k)* in one column and all the words with the *angry* cat (s) in the other column. He then draws a picture next to each word to show he knows what it says.

This use of associative recognition followed by categorizing by manipulative approach lends reinforcement through active learning, as opposed to the usual testing, which is the effect of most workbook exercises.

Chapter 11

Auditory/language memory

ATTENTION AND CONCENTRATION

CHILDREN with visual perceptual problems learn by listening. Their academic potential is often judged by their exceptionally good verbal intercourse during class sessions, their good vocabulary, their quickness to grasp a concept, and their excellent home projects (manipulative and creative works). These children are the ones who make the "careless" errors on their daily papers because of inadequately operating attention and concentration circuits, poor visual function, or poor visual perceptual skills.

Most disturbing to the teacher, the parent, and to such a student himself, however, is his poor performance on weekly tests. The answer is often, "He didn't study," or "He isn't trying." This may not be the situation at all.

Test profiles may show that auditory perception (receptive and expressive) is average to well above average, but that auditory memory is below that expected for the child's age or his intellectual norm. It is this often very large discrepancy of several years between understanding what is said and retaining what is heard that causes the problem seen in poor test grades and elsewhere.

Studying harder or for a longer period does not seem to effect any change in recall, other than possibly in immediate memory. A change in approach *can* affect long-range recall. One method has been found to be, above all others, a very successful attention focuser that requires concentration and results in long-term memory. This method involves the associative picture clue utilized in pictogramming® material to be studied. The method can be used with any academic subject at any grade level, as well as in the adult world.

PICTOGRAMMING

Pictogramming is, in essence, the use of an associative picture to clarify meaning of what is learned from reading. It requires concentration, tapping the good visual memory for meaningful stimuli and thus boosting retention. Examples of the uses of associative pictures have been given throughout this book. In those examples, the student is asked to provide a meaningful picture that will offer him a strong clue to aid recall of a word or symbol.

Pictogramming, as developed by the authors, is used for students from about fifth grade upward who show difficulty retaining what they learn in their content subjects.

At this point, their pictures must reflect an exact and clear meaning of the word(s) read which should be taken from direct context. The following procedures must be followed step-by-step, as pictogramming is not as easy to do properly as an associative word picture. Like other methods, to gain the greatest benefit, it must be used properly.

Provide a simple text such as *New Practice Readers* by Webster* in which a vocabulary list is provided for words used in the immediate context.

Provide 3" x 5" file cards. On the lined side have the students write the word to be defined. On the other side they will draw their pictogram. They must learn to visualize from a specific context which is provided for them. For example, the word *cured* is used in a sentence: "The doctor cured the sick woman with a shot of penicillin." *Cured* could be pictogrammed as illustrated.

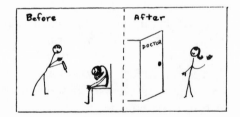

If a child were preparing a Pictogram of the verb to *chart,* as in, "He wanted to chart his course," he would have to express, "The person is working with a map or graph, as well as something which is being plotted, mapped, or graphed. In

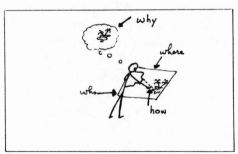

Pictogram of "to chart"

---

*NEW PRACTICE READERS, Webster Division, McGraw Hill, Inc., St. Louis, 1962.

addition, he needs a tool for this work." (Encourage the child to use stick figures and to be brief but accurate in his information.)

Dictionary definitions can be more meaningful with pictograms, particularly for words which have more than one meaning. Present each word to the child in an illustrative sentence *before* the dictionary is checked.*

For example, illustrate the word *once*.

The queen bee uses her wings only *once*.

Once the queen bee gets her wings she can fly.

Once upon a time the bee had no wings.

Have the child pictogram each. Now go to the dictionary and match meanings to each pictogrammed sentence.

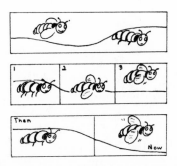

Practice at this level until the child becomes quick and proficient in getting at the essentials of the meaning as used in the specific context he is reading. In order to do this, he must cover the following points:

WHERE. All pictograms must begin with *where*. The *where* must be accurately illustrated. This would be especially important in studying history or geography. If the term is geographic and the child has only a vague map knowledge, he would have to look up the location and copy the shape as well as the proper spatial referent. For example: *nomad* — "The nomad tribes of North Africa roam the Sahara Desert most of the year following a food source. They have no fixed home."

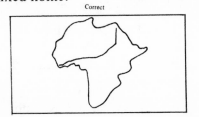

*This story and illustration are reprinted from Norma Banas's and I. H. Wills's book, *Success Begins With Understanding*, p. 21, with the permission of Academic Therapy Publications.

The *where* may be a physical location that is not geographic, as in science texts. Example: *heart —* "The heart is a hollow muscular organ which pumps and circulates our blood at approximately one beat a second." The *where* is not specified, but it is the student's responsibility to seek out the *where* and set the stage for his pictogram.

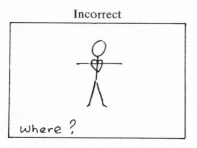

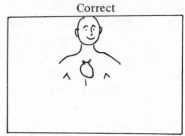

Who or What. Obviously one cannot know what he is talking about if he cannot specify who or what. This is trickier than it would appear and often children cannot isolate the key or main idea of the topic, paragraph, or sentence. Once they know the subject, it still remains somewhat tricky to visualize its essence. For example:

Nomads — what are they? (people)

heart — what is it? (a muscle)

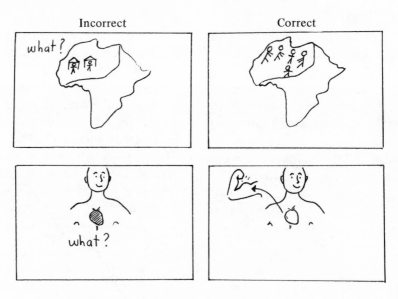

When. When can be as simple as a date of an event or a period of time specified by a set of dates, to a nonspecified time which is inferred (past, present, or future). It can be found by words following key (adverbial phrases) prepositions. For example: In the summertime, after dark, most of the year, approximately one beat per second.

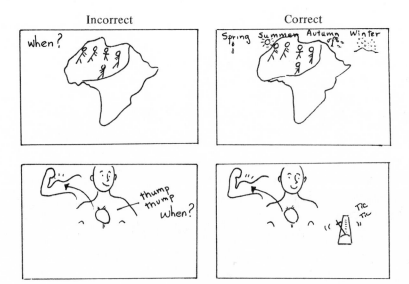

Incorrect   Correct

How. How is not always a part of the context being studied, and therefore may not be a part of all pictograms. It is unfortunate that only the essence is taught without the cause and effect. This is one reason that a great deal of what is learned are rote definitions lacking real meaning and thus preventing transfer of learning. Nevertheless, the student does not have to include in his pictogram the *how* if he is not required to know this. If it is, however, specified or even implied, it then must be included. For example, in the nomad segment, a picture accompanying the text may show men on camels, or previous knowledge would supply this information.

In the heart segment, the how is implied by the word *pump.*

Why. Why is a question requiring probably the most depth of thinking. It may be stated direction ("... following a food source"); yet, if asked, "What does this really mean," or "Why do they have to follow a food source?" one is surprised at the lack of clarity or even awareness of the concept implied.

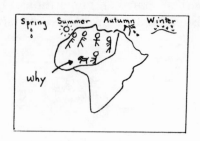

"The heart... circulates the blood" is equally a *how* answer, yet this does not lead us to understand what would happen if this were not done.

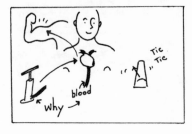

The pictogram illustrates this context accurately; however, by the very vagueness of the context we are reading at times, some essential end results or cause/effect may be omitted. A thorough teacher can see from the pictogram where essential thoughts or concepts can be developed and added.

The *where, who/what, when, why,* and *how* sequence should be followed (in this order) with *all* levels of pictogramming. Once this sequence is practiced with specific words in context and becomes easy to handle and is properly done, the next step is to use pictogramming with a science text.

In science, the important words will be found in bold face or italic type. The students are directed to these words (one at a time) and follow the same procedure as described above. In science the context is usually complete and fully presented, as the very purpose is to clarify new concepts and terms. The students must read the sentence in which the word is contained, and the sentences just before and after. He will often find illustrations, but must not use the illustration provided. This would not tell us, nor him, that he really understood the principal expressed by the term he is pictogramming. Example: *asteroids* — "tiny planets whose paths of revolution around the sun lie between the orbits of Mars and Jupiter. More than 1500 of these have been discovered. Some of them are a few hundred feet in diameter."

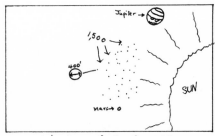

pictogram of "asteroid"

Students should pictogram all terms in bold type, in italics, or those listed at the end of the chapter. If he does this as they are presented in class, he will find he covers a few each day as he moves through the text. The pictograms now become his test review material. He is to take out the cards pertaining to the material to be covered on a test and, (1) look at the word side and guess the picture, or (2) look at the picture side and guess the word.

The next step is to be able to pictogram in a history, government, civics, or social studies text. This is not nearly as easy as in a science text and requires a lot more selective reading and interpretive thinking. Most of these texts are not laid

out with italicized words, nor are
terms specifically defined and illustrated (though some may be). Instead, the key words or terms may
be chapter or paragraph headings,
and the entire following text may
contain the essence of the meaning
of the term. Still, a term must be
summarized concisely. For example, "Reconstruction" (following the Civil War) could be summarized in a pictogram as illustrated.

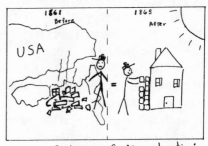

Pictogram of "Reconstruction"

Pictogramming is itself a science. It is a valuable tool to encourage depth
in reading, to direct attention and force concentration, and in so doing, to
build recall.

Vague or incorrect pictograms will reflect vague or incorrect reading
which will lead to vague or incorrect learning and recall. Do not rush the
student in his acquisition of this skill. It can be a valuable tool for the rest of
his life.

Pictogramming has been used to learn foreign language vocabulary (words
and phrases), to learn upper level math concepts, and to aid adult studies as
for real estate examinations, machine operation, or sewing procedures.

Chapter 12

Language development: auditory/visual matching

FACTORS such as attention span, discrimination, direction-al/sequential organization and perception of auditory stimuli have been covered in the preceding chapters. Auditory intake can be adequate, yet conventional exposure and experiences have not been effective in developing language visualization that is accurate for communication and for learning from listening or reading.

One of the little-recognized interfering factors is that *visual* perception (making meaning from visual stimuli) may be deficient and that because of less-than-accurate *visual* perception, many auditory/visual mismatches occur and language development is affected.

We learn language as labels for three-dimensional objects, for pictures, and for abstracts or concepts in our world. If the child is not able to recognize and organize the visually oriented world, he cannot be expected to attach its labels with accuracy and is seen as having a "language disability," when in reality he has a visual perceptual lag.

Vocabulary training and conventional methods for language development have thus often failed to effect the changes and development desired. This may be because of the unrecognized *visual* perceptual deficiency which was behind the language disability. When training is initiated which is oriented to the development of visual perception and accurate auditory/visual matching, the child will often be seen to make significant gains in learning.

Language is a code to relate what we see (an object, a picture, a symbol) or experience (feel). Some children can learn a large number of words and their definitions (vocabulary); but can they match them to the proper referent? If the child can verbalize with the three-dimensional world, can he do the same with the linear, two-dimensional representation? If he can work with the meaningful world, can he handle symbols? If he can give an appropriate verbal response for a visual stimulus, can he visualize (picture in his mind) the experience from verbal stimuli?

Manipulative experiences in learning and in the acquisition of words are therefore essential. (The visual clue in picture form can be used if the perceptual deficiency is not interrupting the perception of linear stimulus.)

Recall of a label does not imply communication will be adequate for the learning process. Many children obtain high vocabulary scores and can do well on tests which require rote recall of facts, names, dates, etc.

Can these same children use language in communication? Do they receive an accurate visualization (visual or mental image)? Can they organize data presented verbally (either orally or in written form)? Can they see inferences and verbalize the content?

For some children all, or a combination of, approaches will be necessary before they can internalize and use what is being taught through language.

The child who cannot visualize from language cannot hold or visualize from nonstatic presentation and must have his language training presented with static visual models upon which to hang recall; or he may need manipulative, three-dimensional experiences before he can accurately visualize the use of labels and the meaning of words.

With heterogeneous group instruction, presentation and reinforcement using each of the activities in all sections would be advised.

GENERAL RULES FOR TEACHING LANGUAGE

1. Immediately reinforce in context after introducing a new word or concept.
2. Simultaneously provide the spoken (or written) word and the experience or object it represents.
3. Associate words with their concrete or manipulative counterpart, *then* move to the pictorial two-dimensional representation.
4. Numerous and varied experiences must be provided to establish broad application and transfer in the use of newly learned words and concepts.
5. Personal experiences should precede common labels and associations, and be internalized before approaching abstract and non-personal environment.
6. Concepts must be taught, not labels alone (e.g. a chair is furniture).

COLORS

Sorting – A Manipulative Associative Experience

Materials

Colored discs, ten of each color (red, orange, yellow, green, blue, purple), and six individual containers colored to correspond to the color of the discs.

Procedure

(1) Start with the primary colors. Working as a group with teacher leading, pick up a colored disc and place it into proper container, naming the color. The children listen, see, and copy for a total reinforcement of correct response to avoid trial and error.

(2) Next add the discs of one secondary color, then another until all colors are covered.

(3) Soon the children can work in pairs without the teacher as a leader.

Concentration: An Auditory/Visual Matching Experience

Materials:

3″ x 5″ cards cut in half, one side white, one side colored, two of each color.

Procedure:

(1) Shuffle the cards. Place them face down on the table in two rows.

(2) Play Concentration, naming the color as each card is turned over. When a pair is found, the player keeps it. Continue until all cards are claimed.

Matching: A Manipulative Associative Exercise

Materials

3″ x 5″ card, cut in half. One each:
white, yellow, orange, red, green,
blue; blank on one side, color name
on reverse side.
Set of white cards: blank on one
side, color name on reverse side.

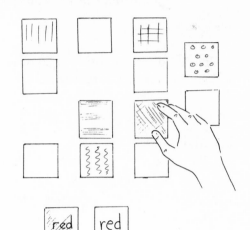

Procedure

(1) Shuffle both sets of cards and
    place them word side down on
    the table in two rows.
(2) Play Concentration by match-
    ing a color card to the white
    card of the same name.

Materials

Key card as illustrated; 3″ x 5″
cards cut in half.
Set of white cards with a color
name on one side.
One set of white cards with color
spot crayoned on one side.

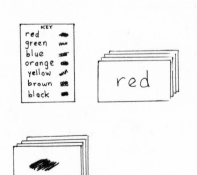

Procedure

(1) Find color on key card. Note
    color name next to it.
(2) Find that color word and put it
    with the proper color-marked
    card.
(3) Continue until all are paired.

Variation

(1) Shuffle the word cards.

(2) Taking the color-marked cards one at a time, find the color name next to each on the key card.

(3) Take the proper crayon and copy (using the crayon) the word on a piece of paper, saying its name.

(4) Continue until all words are written.

(5) Next, shuffle the color word cards and find out what each says by referring to the key card. Then follow the same procedure as in (3).

(6) Then, shuffle both word cards and color-marked cards together and follow the same general procedure.

BODY PARTS

What's Missing? A Manipulative/Associative Game

Materials

Thirty pictures: ten each of a person facing front, facing sideways, and facing backward, each with various parts missing.

Set of missing parts cut out individually to fit in each picture.

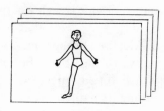

Procedure

(1) The teacher calls out the name of a part and points to the picture.
(2) The child finds the missing piece, names it, and places it on his picture.

Coloring Fun

Materials

Crayons and a drawing of a person.

Procedure

(1) The teacher calls out the name of a part of the body pointing to it on the picture.
(2) The child then colors that part on his paper.

Bingo: Auditory/Visual Matching

Materials

Magazine; paper divided in sixteen parts, enough blanks for each child to use in playing Bingo.

Procedure

(1) Children cut out pictures of sixteen parts of the body. Allow them to use any appropriate pictures so that selection varies.

(2) Paste one picture into each of the sixteen boxes on his paper (to make a Bingo card).

(3) The teacher calls out a name of a part of the body.

(4) The child covers it with his blank if it is on his card.

(5) Continue until someone has all of a row across, down, or diagonally covered and calls, "Bingo." Check.

Variation

The teacher may say, "Cover a part of the body that is on top of your neck" (head).

Pin the Leg on Me: A Manipulative/Associative Game

Materials

Trace two drawings around the child as he lies on the floor on a piece of brown paper. Cut one up into various recognizable body parts.

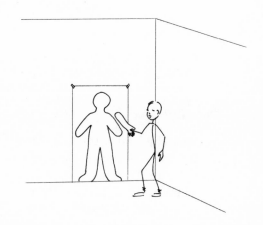

Procedure

(1) Pin the total outline drawing on the wall so that the feet touch the floor.

(2) Teacher, or partner, calls out the name of a body part.

(3) Children find it among their pieces and tape it over the place on the large outline.

Variation

Children fill in their features and clothing by examining their own bodies, then relating to their paper.

The Doll Makers: A Kinesthetic Experience

Materials

Profile Pete (Open Court Pub. Co.), Moveable Melvin (McGraw-Hill Book Co.)

Procedure:

(1) With the teacher, the children assemble a man naming the parts as they are added.

(2) Next they may add clothing and features, discussing where items go, e.g. "The belt goes on his waist. The socks go under the shoes up to his ankle."

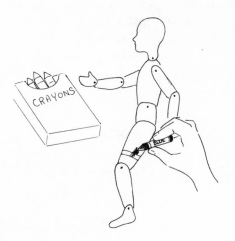

Simon Says: A Verbal/Kinesthetic Game

Materials

None

Procedure

The child must touch each part of the body as the teacher calls it. At first, the teacher may have to touch his body as he says its name.

NUMBERS

Numbers are very abstract and the sound attached to each symbol is an arbitrary assignment. Children may have good number concepts (know what constitutes one item, two items, etc.), yet not be able to recall the name of the number symbol.

Associative Number Pictures

Materials

Pictures should be made that provide a mnemonic clue for each of the digits 1 to 10, as follows:

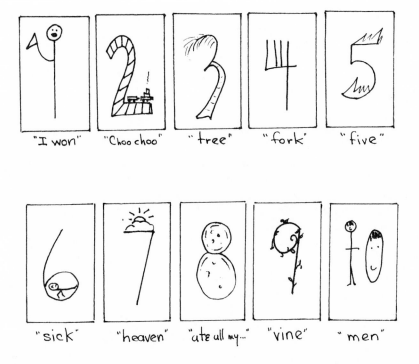

"I won"   "Choo choo"   "tree"   "fork"   "five"

"sick"   "heaven"   "ate all my..."   "vine"   "men"

Procedure

These associative pictures are to be placed on the child's desk to be referred to as he works.

Bingo

Materials

Bingo sheet with sixteen spaces. Ten spaces are numbers 0 to 9; the remaining six spaces are the words for the numbers 1 through 6.

Procedure

Same as previously instructed.

BINGO			
1	9	3	6
three	5	five	two
one	six	2	7
4	four	8	seven

Concentration

Materials

Set A – Paired cards containing the numbers 0 to 9.
Set B – Paired cards of symbol and number quantity as expressed by objects.
Set C – Paired cards for numbers and number words 0 to 9.

SET A 2 = 2

SET B 2 = ⊘ ⊘

SET C 2 = two

Procedure

Same as previously instructed.

ACTION WORDS

Bingo: An Auditory/Visual Activity

Materials

Bingo sheet with sixteen spaces on which are pasted sixteen pictures, cut from magazines, of actions.

Procedure

Same as previously instructed.

Concentration: An Auditory/Visual Activity

Materials

Set A – Paired cards containing simple drawings of actions.
Set B – Pictures cut from magazines of ten different actions. Find the same ten actions in different pictures (same action but nonidentical pictures). Paste each on a 3″ x 5″ file card.

Procedure

Same as previously instructed.

Pantomine: A Kinesthetic Experience

Materials

Cardboard person, with limbs connected by paper fasteners so they are moveable.

Procedure

(1) The teacher effects a pose and the children copy the action by placing their cardboard person into the same position. The children try the pose and name the action. If they cannot visualize from a nonmoving position, the teacher does the action (hop, run, etc.) and the children name it.

(2) The teacher arranges his cardboard person into various postures. The children copy and name the posture (sitting, walking).

SHAPES
Bingo

Materials

Bingo sheet with sixteen squares; ditto sheets with lined drawings of a square, rectangle, circle, oval, triangle, cross, *t*, cube.

Procedure

(1) Have children find pictures from the magazine utilizing each of these shapes (an apple is round).
(2) Cut out lined drawings and magazine pictures and paste on Bingo sheet.
(3) Play as usual, but two places will be covered each time (line drawing and corresponding object).

Concentration

Materials

Use the pictures from the ditto sheets used in Bingo. Find in a magazine a new set of pictures to correspond with each of the shapes.

Procedure

(1) Cut out and paste each picture and ditto drawing on a separate 3″ x 5″ card.
(2) Play as previously outlined.

Hidden Shapes

Materials

3″ x 5″ card with each of the shapes from the ditto pasted on them (one to a card). 8 1/2″ x 11″ pictures (taken from a magazine, children's coloring book, or drawn by the teacher).

Crayon or wax pencil.

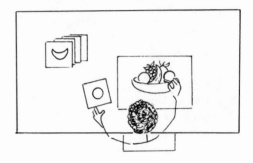

Procedures

(1) The teacher calls out a shape. Each child finds the corresponding 3″ x 5″ card illustrating it.

(2) Using the 3″ x 5″ card as a visual referent, the children are to find and trace all parts in their picture that have this shape.

(3) The children compare with each other and discuss.

CLOTHING

Bingo

Materials

For Bingo using articles of clothing.

Procedure

Play as previously instructed.

Variation

Teacher may call, "Cover any piece of clothing worn by a boy (girl, baby, etc.), to go to bed, (go to school, etc.)."

Color Fun

Materials

(1) Pictures of persons emphasizing clothing.
(2) Crayons.

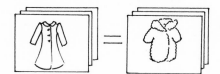

Procedures

(1) The teacher calls out the name of an article of clothing.
(2) The children color the appropriate part of the picture.

Concentration

Materials

3" x 5" cards
Cut from magazines ten different pictures of clothing. Now find ten additional pictures of the same

piece of clothing in each of the first ten pictures, but not an identical picture. For example, two pictures will be included of a blouse, or pajamas (can be boy's or girl's, adult's or child's), etc., so that matching is by the concept involved, not by shape. Paste one each to a file card.

Procedure

Same as previously instructed.

To continue to learn the names of objects in the environment, follow the procedures previously explained for Bingo, Color Fun, and Concentration.

The following list of suggested topics to cover will vary with the need of the child, but offer coverage that will be used for reading and listening comprehension.

Naming	*Related Topics*
animals	foods they eat
fish	parts of animals
birds	habitats (natural and man-made)
insects	animal products
plants	plant produce
foods	source of foods
natural phenomena	natural products
types of buildings	building parts
	rooms
	indoor furnishings
	outdoor implements
people	toys
	musical instruments
	sports and play activities
	occupations
	emotions
vehicles	surfaces
	sites

POSITION WORDS

Obstacle Course

Materials

Set up classroom or play area with chairs, tables, ladders, waste baskets, boards, or whatever is available at hand.

Procedure

(1) Follow-the-Leader is played but the leader and all the followers must verbalize as they execute the course. "Go over the board, go around the chair, crawl under the table, etc."

(2) Command Performance is played by a leader calling out instructions which are followed by the class. First, a single instruction is given, then a series.

(3) Charades is played by a student performing a single action, then a series, and having the class call out what he is doing.

Variation

Show a picture clearly illustrating an action or a series of actions and have the children copy this action. They must always verbalize what they are doing.

Concentration

Materials

Make 3″ x 5″ cards containing paired *but not identical* pictures of positions.

Procedure

As usual, verbalize each action/ relationship as card is turned over.

Variation

Make a set of 3″ x 5″ cards with pictures illustrating action/relation-ships (child *on* a horse, dog going *into* a house). Make a second set containing the words to express the action/relationship of the picture cards.

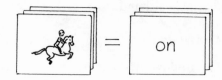

Procedure

Play as usual, but match picture and word.

Guess What?

Materials

Have each child find five pictures in a magazine to illustrate each of the position words found on the key cards (see the illustration fol-lowing).

Procedure

In turn, a child holds up one of his pictures and says, "It is some-thing that is on top of a hill (or whatever is appropriate). Can you guess what it is?"

Bingo

Materials

Make a set of key cards for each child, as illustrated. Make sheets for Bingo using sixteen pictures cut from magazines or lines drawn which illustrate position words.

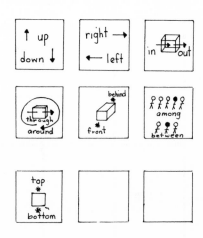

Procedure

Blank keys should be used to introduce any appropriate or desired groups not presented above. Proceed as usual, but have key cards available for children to refer to as they work.

Fun With Words

Teach the children that we do not always want to use position words. Many things in our world have specific names which tell us the same information. These words are so specific that they let us use fewer words to tell someone where to look. For example, instead of saying, "It is on top of the house," we can say, "It is on the roof." Examples of words which refer *to the top of* are *lid, roof, ceiling.*

Illustrate each word with a drawing, then have each child find several pictures and cut them from a magazine. Let the children discover how to apply these words. For example, "A lid can be on a . . .?"

Booklets can be made showing the use of these words. Make a page for each word. Center the term, *lid,* and encircle it with pictures of objects which have a lid on them.

RELATIONSHIPS

short	tall	long	near	far	small
large	little	big	thick	thin	alot
heavy	light	fat	more	less	least
most	many	few	much	-er	-est

Materials

Make a set of picture key cards, as illustrated. Make a ditto sheet of words, as above.

Procedure

(1) Cut out the word cards and match them to each picture key to show the correct relationship.

(2) Add more words and build relationships with objects within the classroom.

(3) Introduce the use of -er and -est and build words and show relationships with these new words. Go as far as desired for the needs of your pupils.

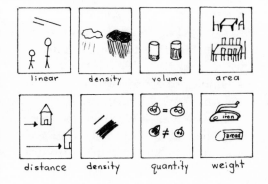

THE SENSES

wet	dry	moist	damp	soggy
hard	soft	rough	smooth	slippery
sweet	sour	bitter	hot	cold
loud	soft	harsh	squeeky	sudden
rubbery	sad	happy	silky	ringing

Materials

Make a set of picture key cards, as illustrated. Make a ditto sheet of words, as above.

Procedure

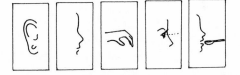

(1) The children bring to class foods and materials to taste, smell, etc. They then close their eyes and identify the item with whatever sense they need to use to do so. Relate each to one of the senses by sorting to the key pictures.

(2) Cut out magazine pictures of things that have a specific taste, smell, etc., and make into a bulletin board display by surrounding each of the key pictures with appropriate pictures.

(3) Assemble sets of pictures which show that some of our descriptive words come from the name of the object itself (rubbery from rubber) or from the action used (ringing sound).

(4) Cut out the word cards. Find pictures to illustrate each of the word cards and sort to the appropriate key.

(5) Discover new words and find pictures for each; sort to key.

(6) Sort word cards to keys without picture aids.

(7) Use these words in sentences or in a pantomine game.

FAMILY RELATIONSHIPS

Materials

Make the two key cards shown. Make a ditto sheet of the family tree and word slips as illustrated on page 200.

Procedure

(1) Sort each word slip under the proper picture key to show which words refer to a boy and which refer to a girl member of a family.

(2) Pass out the family tree. As a group, with teacher leading, begin at the top of the page and place the word slips for *mother* and *father* on *Mary* and *Joe*. Continue down the chart labeling their children and grandchildren. Remove the word slips.

(3) To help see the meaning of a family tree, play a game of Guess Who? Take turns asking questions such as, "Who has two daughers? Who is not married? Who is an only child?" The one to get the correct answer asks the next question.

(4) Another day, begin with Bill. The children pretend they are Bill. They label Bill's parents and grandparents, using the boy and girl picture key cards and place them on the chart to add another set of grandparents for Bill.

Mary   Joe

Jane   John   Bob

Bill   Tom   Dan

Ann   Sue

| daughter |
| son |
| sister |
| brother |
| mother |
| father |
| wife |
| husband |
| niece |
| nephew |
| aunt |
| uncle |
| cousin |
| grand- |
| great- |
| 1st |
| 2nd |
| in-law |

(5) Remove the word slips. Now label Mary and Joe as mother and father again. This time the children pretend they are John. They must find the correct label to show the relationship to them of Jane and Bob.

(6) As a class, find Jane's husband and label him. Find Bob's wife and label her. Put another label on each of them to show what relationship they are to John. Put another label on Jane and her husband to show what relationship they are to Mary. Put another label on Jane and her husband to show what relationship they are to Sue and Ann.

(7) Find Jane's children and label their relationship to John.

(8) Label John's son. Put another label on John's son to show what relationship he is to Sue and Ann. Find others with this same relationship to each other.

(9) Continue in this way until you have explored all possible relationships.

(10) Another lesson, add *1st* and *2nd* word slips to *cousin* to show what they mean. Add *great* to *aunt* and *uncle* to show its meaning.

PRONOUNS

themselves	it	him	herself	we	ours
himself	she	his	her	theirs	their
ourselves	hers	our	them	they	I
myself	us	mine	your	me	yours
yourself	he	you	my		

Materials

Make a set of picture key cards, as illustrated. Make a ditto sheet of words, as above.

Procedure

(1) Using word cards and the key cards, the children put each word under either the boy, the girl, or the ball picture according to which they refer. (Note that some words will not fit.) Discuss that the word *it* is used with objects, not people or animals, because those have a sex. Of the remaining words, find those that refer to more than one person and place them under the picture of the group of people. (Note that these words are used for either sex or mixed sexes.)

(2) Remove all the word cards. Practice with these words using the children in the classroom. Let them see how they have different names depending upon the changing relationships to another child.

(3) Have each student place his name on the picture above where indicated. Have the students find all the word slips that refer to themselves and place them under their pictures.

(4) Next, have them find all the words which they use when talking to someone else and place them under that picture.

(5) Have each student place his name on the group picture to show that the group includes him. Have him find all the word slips that refer to the group which includes him and put them under the picture.

(6) Next, have each student find all the words which he would use when talking about his group of friends in which he is not found and put them under that group picture.

TIME

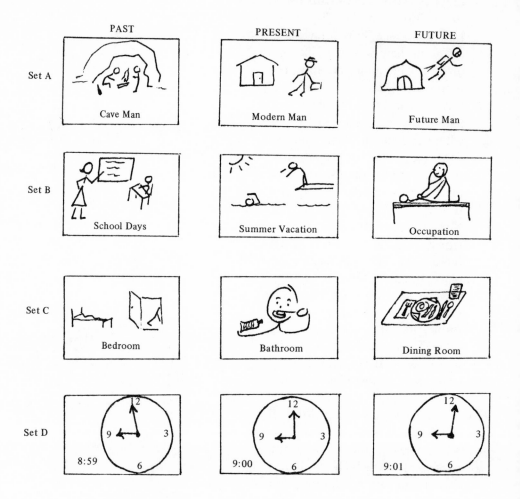

Materials

Make key cards as above.

Procedure

(1) Explore with the students the concept of past, present, and future and how the *length* of time is not the determining factor.

(2) Magazine pictures should be collected for each set of key cards.

(3) Charades should be played acting out an activity and seeing what part(s) relate to past, present, and future and to which set. For example, "Pretend you are baking a cake. You are stirring the batter." Children then decide that the past actions included such things as reading the recipe (set C) and putting in the ingredients (set D). The future action may be the putting of the batter in the oven (set D), taking it out when done (set C), and then the eating of the cake (set C).

THE CALENDAR

Days of the Week

Materials

Make ditto sheets as illustrated on the next page. Give one to each child. Have them cut out the word slips containing the names of the days of the week.

Procedure

(1) On the blank calendar put a sun in one of the boxes, any box. Call that space a "day."

On the same line as the sun, they fill in the other boxes with clouds, rain, snow, or sun. Call these days a "week."

The week begins with Sunday. The children place their word cards at the top of the calendar over the abbreviation for each of the days of the week.

Practice sequencing the days of the week by arranging the week day name slips in order, then checking to the top of the calendar.

SUN.	MON.	TUES.	WED.	THURS.	FRI.	SAT.

January	February	March	April	May	June
31	28	30	30	31	30

July	August	September	October	November	December
31	31	30	31	30	31

SUNDAY	MONDAY	TUESDAY	WEDNESDAY	THURSDAY	FRIDAY	SATURDAY

HOLIDAYS AND SEASONS

Cut out the month holders and fold on the dotted lines.

Halloween	Lincoln's Birthday	Valentine's Day
Easter	Memorial Day	Washington's Birthday
Mother's Day	Father's Day	St. Patrick's Day
Thanksgiving	Columbus's Birthday	Independence Day
Christmas		

Months

(2) Begin with any box in the top row of the calendar. Put in the number 1. Number each box in order (be sure the children always return to the left side of the page when they move to the next line), from 1 to 31. Students will get to the last box and discover that there are not enough spaces to finish to 31. Explain that a month has an uneven number of weeks. Add the necessary extra boxes and finish numbering them to 31.

"On what day of the week does this month end? On what day of the week will the next month begin? Do any months have just four weeks? Do any months have more than five weeks? Add the number of weeks from each month. How many weeks are in a year?"

Holidays and Seasons

(3) The children cut out the picture and name cards of the holidays and seasons. Then they cut out the month cards and count them. There are twelve months in a year. Note the different numbers of days in each month.

Get a calendar which shows the major holidays. Beginning with January, have the children find the holidays which they have on their picture cards. (You may add others if you wish.)

They put the holiday cards with the month cards until all twelve months are covered.

With the teacher, the children discuss and match each holiday name to its picture and find out what the weather is like at that time. Color the picture cards by the following code:

> sunny *summer* days — red,
> cool *fall* or *autumn* days — brown,
> crisp, cold *winter* days — blue,
> breezy, rainy *spring* days — green.

You should find that the red holiday cards fall within the months of July and August and most of September. The brown cards fall within the months of October and November and most of December. The blue cards fall with the months of January and February and most of March. The green cards fall within the months of April and May and most of June.

Note that, although Christmas will be considered by the children as a blue, winter month, it falls into December which belongs primarily as a brown month. This will lead to the discovery that the beginning of the season falls near the end of a month, thus a season chart would have four months which are two colors each.

Returning to the month cards, the children color them *on the back* by the season code above.

Let the class practice sequencing the month cards to the seasons. Turn over the month cards and check by color. Practice sorting the holiday to its month. Always keep a well-marked calendar available to which they may refer.

Prescriptive Teaching

FEELINGS

bored	worried	mad	disinterested
happy	afraid	glad	frightened
cheerful	anxious	sad	discouraged
annoyed	fearful	love	surprised
nervous	gloomy	fond	troubled
unhappy	angry	scared	impatient

Materials

Make a set of picture key cards, as illustrated. Make a ditto sheet of words, as above.

Procedure

(1) The top two faces in the illustration represent positive and negative feelings. Each of the pictures below these faces can be sorted to either the positive (happy) face or to the negative (sad) face. Discuss, "How does he feel? What might make him feel this way?"

(2) The children can find pictures from magazines to represent more happy or sad situations and match them to the faces.

(3) They then sort each word slip below to either the happy or the sad face. Show how many words can be used in a similar way. Add new words.

(4) Have the children match the pictures with the word slips and discuss their work.

Chapter 13

Concepts for listening and reading

CONCEPTS FOR LISTENING AND READING

BEING ABLE to give the name for an object does not mean that the child is able to use words meaningfully or accurately. He must be able to see relationships expressed by words, have a knowledge of opposites and of synonyms, and develop concepts and words to discuss appearance, composition, function, origin, and classifications.

Initially, training in reading is concerned with building a sight vocabulary and word attack skills with the aim of recognizing a large number of words. Reading "words" is not reading, however.

Reading as a communication or a learning tool requires realizing that the words on the printed page are but visual symbols for language, which is a code to transmit information. The words should evoke visual images or emotional responses as they trigger recall of the experiences to which they refer. If they do not trigger any recognition response in us, we either have no stored experience with which to match the words, or we may have a deficiency in the ability to cross over from the visual to the language compartments in our brain and find the proper matches. The need for previously stored experiences makes reading entirely new or unfamiliar data very difficult; yet we too often present text books to be read without first establishing stored visual images and/or experiences for the words.

We may accuse students of reading only what they want to read; "He can read his "hot rod" magazines, but not his history text," as if he does this deliberately. Is it not as true that, because a boy has experienced and seen the ideas that are expressed in his 'hot rod' magazine, he can read it meaningfully and thus enjoyably? But in history, for instance, he has not stored experiences nor sufficient amounts of visual images to make it meaningful.

In addition to storing data in our brain, we must sort and classify the bits and pieces of information in order to make them useful. When we do this meaningfully, we develop concepts, and we read and listen with comprehension.

A concept is a generalization about related data. It is a more or less stable perception. When a child has learned to distinguish cats from other animals, whether the cats are large or small, black, white, or grey, he can apply the word *cat* to a class of ideas. He now has a concept. To this concept is applied a word *(cat)* used previously as a label for a specific furry house pet, but now visualized as having a greater meaning. Reading and listening comprehension requires the ability to know how words are being used at each given incident, and comprehension tells us what type visualization to apply to them.

The ability to conceptualize may be related to the ability or disability to recognize the total from its parts. In a hierarchy of development, can a child (1) recognize isolated data and recognize related data, and (2) can he discover and/or visualize the category into which this data fits?

Recognizing Units

Before classification can be taught, information must be available to choose from. This information is taken from spoken and written word forms and held as memory. It cannot be given through words alone though, as the real use of language is matching words to visual images or experiences. These visual images must be accurate and meaningful.

Present cards on which a figure is illustrated with parts disjointed (but in the appropriate position or relationship). "What would this be if all the pieces were moved together?"

Present cards on which a figure is illustrated with parts scattered at random over the card. "What would this be if all the pieces were in the right position?"

Present cards with an identifiable part on each. "What would our picture be if all these parts were on one card and in the correct position?" (a face)

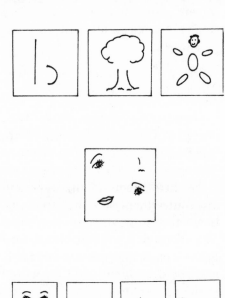

Mix with cards of unrelated pictures. "Find five cards that could be put together to make one picture."

Present cards with an object on each. "These belong to one idea that could tell us a story. What do you think might be happening?"

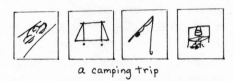

a camping trip

Mix with cards of a different theme. "Make two piles of these cards and tell me why they belong together as you sorted them."

Now introduce word cards which, when grouped, would fit into one category. (cities around the world)

When the children become skilled at classifying, place in the set one card (or more) that is very similar in appearance but different in concept.

Present word cards which will lead to ideas. (a camping trip)

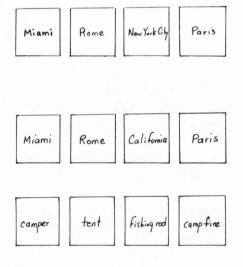

Data can be related in more than one way. Types of relationships are listed in a hierarchy of conceptual difficulty from 1 to 7 on page 217. Make ditto sheets of this type and distribute them to the students. Have the students cut out these classification key cards. Each card shows a particular relationship. This must be discovered and then sorted to the proper key card.

			1. APPEARANCE How do they look? color? shape?
			2. ACTION How do they move?
			3. LOCATION Where are they found? live?
			4. FUNCTION OR USE What do we do with them?
			5. COMPOSITION What are they made of?
finger pencil	bark meow	dress bedspread	**6. SOURCE or ORIGIN** Where do they come from?
turpentine syrup	lamp sun	horn gasoline	**7. CLASSIFICATION** Both are . . . (animals, fruit, etc.)

263

More relationships should be explored with the use of key cards
and pictures to match to each, as
illustrated in the sample worksheet
on page 219. These pictures can be
sorted to several key cards, possibly
for shape similarity, then again for
function similarity, etc. Save classification key cards to use again.

Substitute a paired word set for
classification   sorting.   (Sample
worksheet,   page   220).   Work   to
classification key cards, 1 to 7 from
the worksheet.

Provide sets of cards or a worksheet, as illustrated on page 221.
The individual pictures must be in a
proportion relationship of A is to B
as C is to D. (e.g. *bird, feather,
man, hair.)* Help the student see the
relationship of the first two and
decide what would be the logical
fourth picture. The fourth picture
is then shown.

Provide a sheet of paired pictures, as illustrated on page 222
that suggest different associations.
The particular association must be
discovered and matched to the key
cards 1 to 6.

Cut out all of the squares. Keep the cards with the word on them separate.

Match cards to the word set and explain the relationship. They are alike in that they are made up of the same material . . . etc. Re-sort into other relationships.

Make up more cards for matching or play Go Fish with classmates.

Washington Monument	tricycle	chopsticks
fish	gear	Christmas Tree
Be My Love		

S63

Classify according to the highest function.

Cut out all of the squares. Sort each paired word card to the key card numbered 1-7 that best represents the correct relationship.

For those who can't visualize from the words alone, draw a picture of each word; then sort to the best category that expresses the similarity of each pair.

coal	diamond	dress	bedspread	**1. APPEARANCE** How do they look? color? shape?
finger	pencil	knife	saw	**2. ACTION** How do they move?
paper	bookcase	?	!	**3. LOCATION** Where are they found?　live?
paint	charcoal	marble	gumball	**4. FUNCTION or USE** What do we do with them?
bicycle	windmill	luggage	shoe	**5. COMPOSITION** What are they made of?
string	spaghetti	tire	eraser	**6. SOURCE or ORIGIN** Where do they come from?
fish	submarine	bird	kite	**7. CLASSIFICATION** Both are . . . (animals, fruit, etc.)

RELATIONSHIP cards

Find the relationship of A to B. Now, look at the picture in Column C and decide what would be in the picture in Column D. C-D would have the same relationship as A-B.

A	B	C	D

ASSOCIATIONS

Cut out all of the squares. Sort each paired picture card to the numbered key card that represents the best relationship.

Key Cards

1. opposites

2. cause/effect

3. synonyms

4. partners

5. action/equipment

6. part to whole

CONCEPT DEVELOPMENT: PART TO WHOLE

Since all learning begins from our own experiences and we each interpret what we see and hear according to our own frame of reference, training should begin with one's self.

Since children learn best that which is about themselves, a paper doll family can be developed. Have a child draw his family (father, mother, himself, and any siblings or relatives that are a permanent part of his household, and his major pets). He then pastes his family on cardboard and cuts them out ready to be dressed and played with. Now, it becomes necessary to provide a wardrobe. Again, drawing and cutting will be incorporated, but concept development is involved as we guide the pupil's choice by suggesting a set of outfits for occupation, another set for specific weather, another set for specific activity, etc. Once made, the clothes should be stored in envelopes properly labeled as to their classification (example: Mother's clothes, rainy weather clothes, play clothes, etc.).

As many classifications that suggest themselves should be encouraged. When the child goes to place an item in an envelope, he will discover that there is more than one way to classify. Each envelope should also include a picture clue to its contents as a guide.

When several types of clothing have been explored and made, they should be taken from their envelopes and randomly scattered together on the table. The child now re-sorts them back to the proper envelopes using the labels as a guide.

This activity is then extended to include the building of a home for this family. Individual small boxes can be used to design each room with its doors and windows, and then be put together in different ways to design a home and get a total perception of its part-to-whole structure.

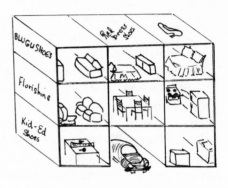

Furniture must now be made to go with the house. To do this, the pupil develops concept and classification of appropriate furniture and furnishings for each room. Each room should be labeled and furniture appropriately sorted.

At the next level of concept development children should make a Language Box containing pictures cut from books of a family, home, clothing, etc. Each should be pasted to a 3″ x 5″ file card for sorting. Work with pictures on cards requires good visual perception. These cards should be placed in a file box behind divider tabs labeled as to the classification. Follow all classification sorting steps as in the activities above. Where an item is found to go in more than one category, a duplicate picture should be provided.

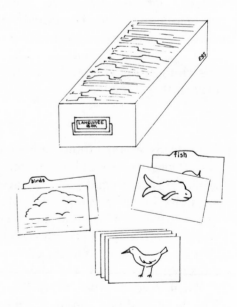

At the highest level of concept development words are substituted for the pictures and sorted in the same way. To do this effectively, the words are put appropriately on the reverse side of each of the picture file card set above. This way, the card can be turned over and checked to insure accuracy in visualizing the word meaning.

The picture/word file box should be expanded to include all important concepts that will be needed in the child's listening and reading experiences. Sets should be made for:

accessories	furniture
animal families	geography
animal food	insects
animal houses	invertebrates
animal parts	mammals
animal products	occupations
birds	people
body parts	phenomena
building parts	plant products
buildings	reptiles
celestial bodies	rooms
clothing	sports
fish	tools
food	toys

Weekly assignments should be made, such as: "Select a category to be learned. For example, domestic animals. Choose *one* alternate category within the same subject, for instance, wild animals found in zoos."

Make a key card for each of the categories and discuss from the child's experience what he knows about each. Always work with a static visual referent when learning relationships. This referent is kept and placed in the file box for use.

Next, either provide a stack of cards containing the pictures of animals for both categories (plus some which will not fit under either heading), or have the children find in magazines pictures of animals for the categories. Check the correctness of choice before pasting the pictures on the file cards. The children sort each picture under one of the categories and discard those that do not fit under either. If errors are made, discuss them; shuffle pictures and re-sort. Have the children bring in more pictures to add to the file for sorting.

Then the children turn to the word side of the cards, shuffle, and match them to the proper headings. They check the pictures to see if their choices are correct.

Add a third category, farm animals, and follow the same procedure. Add a fourth, then a fifth category and so on until all desired possibilities are covered. As categories are added, it will be noticed that some animals can be found in more than one place (farm and home) and new concepts will develop.

When the students are more advanced, categories can be subdivided; for example, transportation can be subdivided into rail, water, land, people, cargo, etc. Food can be divided into prepared or fresh; of animal or vegetable origin.

The teacher can divide the cards into categories and the children explain why they are so placed. This exercise is for the more advanced students and the categorization should be more difficult. Animals might be divided between invertebrates and vertebrates, or even between the better known phylae, or mammals between families. Real thought about the properties of the animal is required.

To increase visual perception and meaning vocabulary, provide ditto sheets following specific categories, such as children from other lands, birds, etc.

Build concepts for the object(s) in the picture for that day through discussion. Talk about color, shape, purpose, size, texture, etc.

The children color the ditto picture. Be sure that the correct color is used. At first, issue only the necessary crayons. Later, let each child have the entire pack from which to choose his colors. It is important to the language and concept accuracy that the children use the correct colors. For example; in the category, children of other lands, the Indian boy must have brown skin color in all flesh areas; the Pilgrim boy's clothes must be in black and white; the Eskimo clothing is fur colored, etc. Incorrect coloring must be immediately corrected by the child to insure proper concept formation.

The children cut out and paste the main object onto a sheet of background paper. They make the picture, color it, and cut out an appropriate environment to build accurate concepts of life style. Example: Put a tree limb under the bird, a nest on the limb, bugs crawling on the limb for the bird to eat, etc. At first, instruct the pupils as to what to place in the picture (do not use paste) as the object's environment. Make the addition simple to visualize for them by drawing it on the board. Later, encourage the children to visualize from previous knowledge what environment is needed.

Remove the items and store in envelopes marked with appropriate classifications: habitats or shelters, food source, etc. These items will grow as subjects are explored and are to be used over and over in rebuilding pictures showing proper matching of information on each subject picture.

LISTENING MEANINGFULLY

Listening meaningfully requires stored information in the form of visual images for words, which can be brought forth appropriately as triggered. Listening meaningfully precedes reading meaningfully.

Inferential thinking, logical conclusions, as well as concept building, are really only part-to-whole abilities based on quickness in seeing the total (overview or gestalt) from minimal clues (details).

Start telling a simple nursery rhyme or sentence familiar to the child. Stop; have the child supply the missing word or concept.

The teacher reads a story and stops at a certain point, showing slightly different pictures to the child; the child picks out the correct one. For example, "The house had a red roof and was in the country." Pictures could be of a house with a green roof, a house with a red roof in the city, etc., only one picture being exactly as mentioned in the story. (For auditory/visual matching, the child has the pictures in front of him and picks out the right one when the teacher mentions that part of the story.)

Extend the topic to familiar or just studied content material for the older student. Stop and have students fill in proper endings. This helps as a review of information and acts like fill-in-the-blank tests.

Use with fictional stories, as in English literature. The teacher reads a story and stops at certain points to question what is reasonable to happen next. There is not necessarily one "correct" answer. For example, the teacher reads, "A boy starts climbing a tree. He has one shoe untied and loose." The teacher then asks the student, "What do you think will happen?" Appropriate answers might be that the boy slips and falls, or that the shoe falls.

The student's appropriate answer may not be the one written into the story; in that case the teacher says, "Your answer is something that might have happened, but actually such and such happened. If the student's answer was totally inappropriate, the teacher will have to discuss why this was so and ask why he chose it.

Illustrate the idea expressed with a picture to show the logic of it, if the idea was incorrect or if the student was having difficulty. The subject used must be familiar, and previous knowledge must be present to draw from, or a child cannot expect to visualize logically.

Read familiar short stories. Pretend to be in a radio station. As the teacher reads a story, have pupils fill in the sound effects (of trains, animals, people walking, knocking on doors, etc.).

Place a number of objects on the table. Call out a category and see how quickly a student can pick up all the things in that category. For example, "Pick up all the things found in a kitchen. Pick up all the things that fly. Pick up all the

things made of metal." Other students should watch and tell if all items chosen are correct and if all are included that should be. Later, do this with picture cards instead of objects.

Describe a common animal, object, or place to the class as follows: "I am thinking of an animal. He is long and thin in shape; he has no legs or arms. He can be green, black, or other colors. He lives under rocks. He comes out to sit in the sun, etc." The children should guess the animal from as few clues as possible.

A child should then describe an animal for the class (making up a word story requires good language visualization). He should be reminded to include the shape, size, color, and prominant features and to tell where the animal lives, what it does, etc. This should develop into an orderly thinking process.

If the children cannot visualize from the words alone, the teacher can draw while talking, or the children can draw as they listen. This gives the teacher a more specific idea of how the students are interpreting the words used. The children should guess with as minimal a clue as possible. Show a completed picture to confirm the visualization.

Tell a brief descriptive tale.

* * * * *

"The boy went to the store for ice cream.
On the way home he played ball.
He watched men paint a house.
He talked with his friend, Jim.
What did his ice cream look like when he got home?"

* * * * *

Have the students draw to illustrate the story and see how well they followed the sequence.

Verbal absurdities can be used. Have the children illustrate what they heard by picturing the concept. This will point out the inconsistency to them or show the teacher where they are missing information or concepts. "At midnight, when the sun was shining, I went to bed." (Vocabulary concepts are required as well as the ability to visualize the situation.)

At a later step, the child should be able to visualize in his mind, rather than having to draw the situation. Speed in recognition is the aim. The child who cannot attend and make meaningful use of conversation will find learning in the middle grades and above very difficult.

Read to the students from a science text, giving several sentences which form a concept; stop, have them illustrate the concept and the details they heard. For example, the following passage from *Stars*, a Junior Science Book by Phoebe Crosby (1960), might be illustrated as shown. The three steps in this drawing, though illustrated separately for clarity, would, in actuality, be added to one single picture as the student listens to this passage:

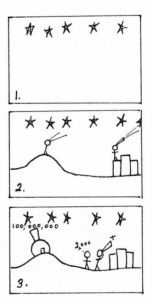

1. "A clear night is the time to see the stars.
2. A hill in the country is a good place. A roof in the city is good, too.
3. In the whole sky you can see about 2,000 stars with your eyes alone. With a pair of field glasses or a small telescope, you can see many thousands more. With the largest telescope, people see hundreds of millions of stars."

Let the students apply this "audiolex" technique as they take notes on the assigned chapter. The resulting pictograms are then a study aid as a means to visualize details, so that an overview is clearly seen, and as a reinforcement to the recall of details. Audiolex is a term applied by the authors to refer to making pictograms from a listening activity. It is excellent training for note taking.

READING MEANINGFULLY

Reading meaningfully is the same as listening meaningfully. However, the eyes must first translate the written symbol into its verbal referent, and the brain must translate the verbal referent into a visual image. This should be an automatic, instantaneous single action. Too often, early reading emphasis is on the identification of the symbols and verbalizing them in their language form. Students can become so involved in the mechanics of decoding that they do not also "read" meaning from the symbols. Early comprehension training is, in reality, memorization of vocabulary words and details, often with no logical structure. "Read and tell me all you remember." Reading meaningfully should be like having a television in one's head. Language, whether verbally or visually "spoken," should always evoke meaningful mental images for the experiences represented by the words.

Following directions requires accurate response to word meanings. A set of duplicator sheets can be made of a lined drawing of an object which is to be completed according to written directions below the picture. Cards should be provided of the finished illustration showing all the necessary additions to the picture to make it complete.

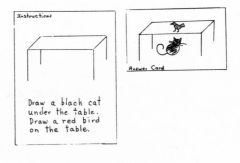

The work when finished should be checked against the model to insure accuracy and completeness.

Make a game of charades out of following directions. Pass out slips of paper (made by the teacher or by pupils) to each child and have him execute the direction. Example:

(1) Close the door.
(2) Say hello to John.
(3) Draw a circle on the board.

Have the rest of the class guess what the child is doing.

Have ditto sheets before each child with similar directions printed

on the sheet. Have pupils illustrate with stick figures each set of directions on their sheet.

Reading to answer the question of identity can be accomplished through duplicator sheets typed on a primer typewriter and answered by choice of a picture. A set of cards should be provided for checking the answers. The question should be on the front of each card and the picture answer with its label on the reverse side. The children can identify the picture answer on the ditto sheet and fill in the name of the object on it. This way they are working on comprehension and vocabulary building at the same time.

On 5″ x 8″ file cards, provide a supply of questions which require information and concepts to answer. Example:

   (1) Is the dog an animal?
   (2) Can a glass break if it falls?
   (3) What happens to the sun after dark?
   (4) Why do we wear clothes?

On the back, illustrate the question so that the child has a reinforcement of his answer immediately, and so that he can see the logic or illogic of the question visually. Store the questions by types (factual, cause/effect, sequence, inference), so that assignments can be made according to the student's need.

Let children make questions for each other to add to the box. Cards may be built from stories in the reader to enhance the understanding of the action and ideas.

Take a simple paragraph and illustrate it sentence by sentence. Each sentence must have the who/what, where, when, why, how (if present) parts illustrated separately. This pictograms the details.

Now, summarize in one picture to show the main idea. All the details are included, but they are related to each other in one pictogram. This relationship of the details (parts) is what should be meant by reading comprehension.

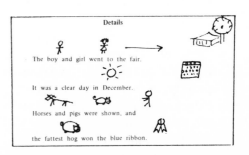

Teach the children to find information rapidly to read to answer specific questions. Children often fail to find the answer to a question quickly, or answer a question with the wrong information because they are not aware of what they are looking for.

Structure is needed. "For what am I looking?" The child must use the five guide questions: (1) where, (2) when, (3) who or what, (4) why, (5) how. He should take one question at a lesson in the order presented above and scan for words to answer that question. Do not let him read word by word. Have the student scan with his finger, moving down the middle of the page, trying to see the words as he goes. For example, "Find all the *where* words." He must learn to look for place words.

(a) New York, Rome, Lisbon, or

(b) on the wall, up the hill, over the fence.

Now he can summarize. "What do we know from these *where* words?"

(a) cities around the world, or

(b) up tall things

Practice daily and take a new question each week until all are easily identified.

For *when* he looks for times, dates, and prepositions, such as *after (dark), before (lunch),* etc. He should learn to be triggered by numerals and calendar words.

For *who* or *what* he would look for nouns, especially proper nouns (capital letters as visual triggers) that refer to people and for objects of any kind. These are very frequent words; therefore, this question cannot be answered as simply as the *where* and *when*. We must now become selective by deciding, "What is the story about?" (title). Now find who/what words that refer to this. Frequency of words triggers us to find the main characters. If *Jane* is seen most often, and another name just once, we conclude the story is about Jane.

For *why* we look for reasons and such triggering words as *because.* For *how* we look for cause/effect and such triggering words as *by* and *through.*

The teacher aids the students in looking for specific details by leading them to understand the kind of answer they are called on to look for. Vocabulary knowledge is, of course, also essential or words will

not be recognized. For instance, if students are told to find the name of the hero, do they know what a hero is?

Increase accurate vocabulary meaning. Several companies have crossword puzzle books, or duplicator sheets in which antonyms, synonyms analytical relations, etc. are employed. The pupils have the benefit of part-to-whole experience as they use meaning vocabulary while reinforcing reading and spelling recognition. A list of the words that will be used should be provided as a clue until efficiency is gained in working from minimal clues and from definitions.

Provide ditto sheets of common phrases that include needed listening and reading key words (vocabulary). Fold paper in half the long way. Provide a key card to remind the students of the use of the guide questions for reading meaningfully and pictogramming. The children pictogram each phrase. Have the class compare and check for accuracy and completeness in expressing the concepts. A complete sentence can be made from each pictogram if it was done accurately. The children should write a sentence under each pictogram.

Introduce the concept of opposites. Set up sheets of paper folded in half, as illustrated, and place one set of opposites on each. The children find more words that show the same general function and place

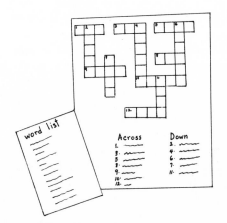

them on the proper sides. Then
they draw a picture to show the
specific meaning of each added
word.

Make a set of twenty cards each
containing one word. Set up and
play a game of Concentration,
matching opposites or synonyms as
desired.

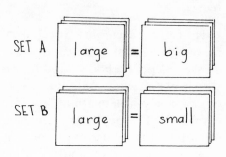

Make a set of opposite flash
cards (do not use words) in pictogram form illustrating one of the
pair of opposites on each side.
Show a card to the class; say the
word or concept *(day);* have them
guess the opposite *(night);* turn the
card over and check. Shuffle the set
and make a list of the words pictogrammed on the facing side. Have
the children guess the opposite
word and list it next to each. Check
the answers.

The difference between a syn-
onym and a category must be
learned, as well as the different
meanings of so-called synonyms.

The synonyms illustrated here
refer to *two,* but not in the same
way. Classifications could be illustrated by:
   cabin
   mansion
   hut
   ranch
   apartment

Word triplicates could be illustrated by:

smart	bright	intelligent
house	home	abode

Have the students make lists of word triplicates and pictogram the differences.

There are many words that are mistakenly or loosely used interchangeably. Choose a category (foods, homes, animals, etc.) and find words which refer to the category and show how, in reality, they have very specific referents.

Too often transfer is not made of the skills taught in isolated practice or learned in workbooks. The child needs to reinforce learning while he works in the areas in which those skills will actually be needed (health, science, social studies, etc.), especially since the books for those subjects are not as simple in structure as the typical workbooks. Too often it is found that the student knows how to handle a task in one situation, but given a slightly altered situation in which to use the same skill, he fails to see the similarity or to apply what he has been taught. The only practical solution is to work in the content areas as soon as the child has gained enough foundation with skills to make this practical.

To enhance the understanding of characters and setting in a literature assignment, have the pupils picture the characters physically. Have them add their impressions of the characters' personalities and show their part in the story. Compare impressions.

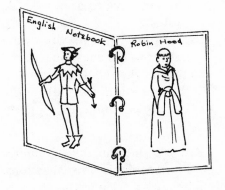

Read aloud from the story and have the children take the parts of the characters. Have them read with the emotion and voice tone of the role. In this way reading is made more meaningful and recall is greatly enhanced. This is an especially appropriate method in upper level literature classes, but role playing is also valuable in any area because the intensification of intake enhances recall.

Repeat this process with history lessons, civics, and government. Dramatizing, plus recreating with pictures or models, will provide visualizations for the words used and enhance understanding.

pictogram of "gravity"

Science, which is related to important people and events, can be pictured and dramatized also. Science data to be learned should be pictogrammed and the word/ picture cards filed for test review.

For history, civics, and similarly structured texts the children should:
> go to the end of the chapter and find the facts questions before reading the chapter.
> write in condensed form each question, one to a 3″ x 5″ file card.
> find in the text, as they read, the answer to the question.
> pictogram the full data to answer the question, including the *who, what, where,* etc.

Reading meaningfully requires good geographic visualizations. Children with a lag in the development of laterality and dominance have a great deal of difficulty with geographic relationships. Whenever geographic locations will be involved in the reading context, puzzle maps should be made. Provide a model to trace. Have students trace, then paste on cardboard, and

cut out the appropriate map segments. Do not write any names on the pieces. From the pieces they should recreate their map, working to a model. A game of identification can be played. Hold up a piece. Have the class guess the name of the area and place it on the model map. Play until all the pieces are placed. The winner is the one who recognized and could place the most pieces on the model.

VOCALIZING MEANINGFULLY

Students must learn to verbalize accurately and meaningfully in expressing information or the words learned as labels have no value. A carefully structured inquiry series is needed to teach them to perceive qualities and give responses in a repeated exposure to language building.

Objects, as realistic as possible for size, texture, etc., should be presented, one at a time. The teacher structures the question/response session, saying: "Describe this to me." Provide the following stimuli questions which the student is to use each time.

1. What color is it?
2. What size is it?
3. What shape is it?
4. What does it feel like?

When a group of five items has been described, ask, "Are any of these items alike in any way?" Lead the students to discover that categories can change (group by color, regroup by shape, regroup by size, then by texture).

Make key cards for each of the four stimulus questions to remind the students of the leading questions and to help the students use them to resort to in categorizing items. Increase the size of the group until sorting and verbalizing is easily handled.

Place a number of objects on the table. The student must guess which one the teacher is thinking of by questioning him. Questioning should follow the guide taught: "Is it round?" Is it green?" etc. The teacher answers only "yes" or "no."

When the student can describe easily, he must learn to look into less tangible qualities which will lead to other classifications.

1. What is it made of? (composition)
2. What can it do? (function)
3. How does it work? (action)

Note that the questions should begin with specific concrete features which are readily observable, and later include inference and perception. Hopefully, each session should require less verbal initiation from the teacher. Again, make a set of key cards and sort and refer to them.

Pictures of objects, pasted on 3″ x 5″ cards should now be substituted for the objects and the process repeated. This requires previous knowledge, stored visual images for the real objects, and visual perception of linear representations.

Pictures of scenes are introduced and the teacher structures the question/response session saying, "Describe this scene."

1. *Who* or *what* do you see? (a boy)
2. *Where* is he? (in a tree)
3. *What* is happening? (picking apples)
4. *When* is this happening? (at noon)
5. *How* is he doing it? (with his hands)

Comprehension of the scene now must be developed. "Tell me about . . ." (Help him to think.)

1. How does he feel?

2. Why does he do it?
3. What steps did it take to get here?
4. What might happen next?

Vocabulary definitions may be obtained from the dictionary and yet have no real value in enlightening the student to their meaning (*internist* — a doctor that specializes in internal medicine). Teachers daily teach new words through context — (You can get a scholarship when you go to college) — and assume the meaning was obvious. When students verbalize vocabulary knowledge, teachers assume again that they really have the correct visual image and meaning.

Ask the student to draw a letter and place an arrow to indicate the part of his picture that refers to the word *letter*. At this point, it is often found that verbalizations of knowledge were not representing accurate visual referents.

Make a picture dictionary to insure accuracy of intake and verbalization of vocabulary.

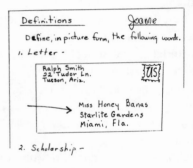

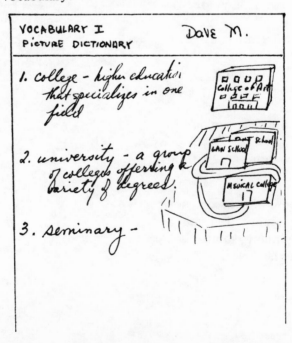

Use of cartoons, captioned or uncaptioned, can increase inferential thinking, notation of details, and information accuracy. A single picture cartoon should be used at first. Ask leading questions to guide the pupil to tell what is happening, why they think this, what do they think will happen next, why, what is the mood of the people involved, etc.

Sequence stories: provide cartoons with few or no words, paste on cardboard, laminate, and cut into individual pictures. Cartoon segments are shuffled and randomly placed in scrambled order facing the student.

The student is asked to look at the segments and guess what they are all about. Seeing or verbalizing a main idea (a summary) seems to be a very difficult task for some students. Usually, the answer tends to be a verbalizing of all the details. In order to perceive the overview and state a generalization, the student must perceive a greater whole from the parts. To do this he must have a good storage of basic information and a great number of concepts into which he can fit the parts.

It has been found helpful to ask the student, "Give me a title for this story." If he cannot do so, offer several titles and allow him to choose the most appropriate one (recognition memory level).

The student is now asked to put the individual segments into major groups. The grouping depends on the subject matter. Suggested divisions might be: before/after/during; inside/outside, etc.

Student now takes the first group of pictures and places them in correct sequence of action. The second group is now put into correct sequence and the groups joined. The student tells the story (he has not yet been told if his sequence is correct), and makes any corrections he finds.

Learning to tell what happened (summarize) without reiterating details is a difficult skill. Try having the students point to and tell what happened in the first picture, "the man was painting," now the last picture, "the man had to take the children out through the window," now the midsection, "because he didn't leave them a way to get across the painted floor."

WRITING MEANINGFULLY

Some students find it easy to verbalize what they know, have heard, or have read (each a more specific skill at a higher level); yet they are not able to put their thoughts into written form.

In some cases they may have this difficulty because the motor skill needed for writing is ineffective or slow and frustrates them too much. In other cases the recall of the visual symbol needed is ineffective or slow. In some cases a mental block toward the writing task seems to be present, and it is avoided or rushed. Writing is so much slower than talking that it is considered boring or tiring by students. For some, the slowing down causes them to lose their train of thought (typing helps). All the skills (motor, visual recall, etc.) involved must be checked so that appropriate remediation can be given.

Special occasions such as holidays, children out sick, etc. can afford an opportunity to make greeting cards, write letters, etc. This is a meaningful, motivating activity, reinforcing skills of spelling and vocabulary through copying and labeling, while a more comprehensive vocabulary is developed.

Write a story on the board to be copied by the pupils onto notebook paper. Use a title which expresses the main idea. Build the story simply, but completely, with student contribution to include who/what, where, when, why, how, to encourage pupils to think in an organized way.

The teacher should encourage the use of words which are proper for the students' grade level, so that they are encountered in other reading situations.

The pupils copy the story from the board and place it in a notebook.

Have each student independently illustrate the story. Share and compare the differences and similarities in interpretation. Place a picture with the story in the notebook.

From the language box, choose a specific number of words and have the child create a story which he will illustrate and read to the class.

To develop creative thinking and writing, give leading questions. "Pretend you are a cat. How would you want to be treated?" Provide ten words which would be helpful in writing this story. These words will give a content clue, as well as aid in spelling and vocabulary.

Show a large picture of an object or an activity. Have the students look at and study the picture. Give the pupils a few minutes to write down as many details as they can about the picture. Guide questions should be placed on the board at first to help collect data in a structured way. Guide questions should include: "How many people are there? What are the people doing? What time is it? Where does this take place?" The students check with each other to see how each perceives the picture. Title it.

Still using the picture and the key words, have each pupil write a brief description of the picture in full sentences. Have them follow the who/what, where, when, why, how, organization, making a paragraph for each.

Sheets should be provided with the needed structure as illustrated on page 253. This is a big help in organized thinking.

Have these descriptions exchanged among the students (a day later) and reillustrate the picture. Have pairs of children see if they correctly described the picture. In this way they can see where improvement on the written description can be made.

The same idea can be used independently. Have each child file his description of the picture until a few days later. Then have him try to match his descriptions with the correct pictures.

Have the children use pictures as a stimulus to write a fiction story. These stories will be read to the class. Following the reading, have each pupil draw an illustration of what he has just heard. The pupils then show their drawings to check against each other's concepts, as well as check with a model.

Write three sentences under each question. Be sure they are complete sentences and have a beginning capital letter and end punctuation for each one.

_____
topic

Who or What?

_____

_____

_____

Where?

_____

_____

_____

When?

_____

_____

_____

Why?

_____

_____

_____

How?

_____

_____

_____

It is fairly easy to invent details for a story, but not that easy to be sure that the sentences truly keep to the topic they are placed with. Phrase cards should be provided and key cards to the headings of who/what, where, when, why, and how, provided. Sort the phrase cards appropriately.

Often, the student cannot write an organized report or story because his initial data is not organized. Thus, writing should follow outlining, which follows intake of data.

Begin with a text such as an encyclopedia. Instruct student(s) to write each fact on a slip as they read, one fact per strip, as illustrated.

Without referring back to the text, the student(s) should arrange the strips into related data. Discuss the various possible arrangements and how categories can vary, yet be equally correct. Now, check to see how the text had organized the facts (by paragraphs) and arrange the strips accordingly.

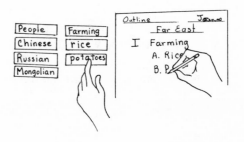

Give each group a heading (if not already present) such as: These five facts are about *farming*.

Discuss and illustrate as a class the outline format. Assign a Roman numeral for each main heading. Place correct fact strips under their appropriate headings and assign a letter of the alphabet to each strip.

Referring to an illustrated outline model, the students should copy their strip outlines onto notebook paper. Check the outlines.

Draw a line between each main idea. For example:

I. Farming
   A. Rice
   B. Potatoes
II. Population
   A. Chinese
   B. Mongolian
   C. Russian

Have each student draw a pictogram for each section illustrating all the details in proper relationship to show that he accurately visualized the text and to aid in long-range recall.

From the phrase outline, the students take each section and write it into complete sentences. Each Roman numeral becomes a paragraph. They add an opening paragraph which is a statement of the question posed by the assignment. "This (report) story is about Russians and how they live." Then they add a closing paragraph which is a summary of what they felt about what they learned. "This reading assignment taught me much new information."

To prepare the child for writing book reports, provide a key card showing who, where, when, and what.

The student should write his book report in the following order:

A. Characters (who)—List the characters and draw a picture depicting each accurately.

B. Setting (where and when) —Draw a picture to show the setting.

C. Plot (what)—Write a summarizing sentence as learned in doing sequence stories. This sentence should state what was the opening action (or state of being), what the closing action (or state of being), and what approach contributed to the change of status.

It is difficult to break the habit of describing the sequence of action. Approach should be taught as to what we are told in our story,

why it happened, how it happened,
etc. Example: Mrs. Jones was mur-
dered. The detective caught the
killer. The story tells how the mur-
derer was caught.

Children who cannot express what they know in writing are at a terrific
disadvantage. The sample of a book report in the illustration below comes
from experience. This fifth grade student had been assigned a book to read
in class. The teacher noted that he was sitting idly and asked why he was not
reading. The student informed her that he had finished the book. The
teacher reacted, "That is impossible, and if so, then write your book report
now." The following written report (done in class) proved to her that he did
not in fact read the book; "It is obvious that this is nonsense."However, at
home, the student read to his parents his written story which, when
translated, showed that he had indeed read and understood the book. If his
teacher had checked him through his exceptionally good verbal channel,
instead of challenging him through his severe deficiency in auditory
discrimination, she would have known that he was learning and had done his
assignment to the best of his ability.

STOCKERS

(Translation of Figure 395.)

There are many kinds of stockers. They are regular cars but with more power. They can reach the speed of 200 MPH. They race on an oval track. They race about 48 cars at a time according to their power.

These cars are just one of the thousands of cars in the world.

IN CONCLUSION

While this text is written primarily for the professional, it is still in point to remember that an informed parent is an important adjunct to a successful learning experience. The authors would like to recommend several books written by and for parents, which offer real, positive and negative learning experiences, which may provide additional insight for the professional.

Can't Read, Can't Write, Can't Takl Too Good Either, by Louise Clarke, is a perceptive personal document of a boy and his family in their quest for guidance, understanding, and therapy. The original diagnosis was one of mental retardation, but the problem, in fact, was a severe perceptual handicap. The story is told with emphasis on how parents (and teachers) can recognize and overcome the effects of dyslexia on a child, following him from his early childhood, through years of school trauma and triumphs, to successful adulthood. The story is very worth reading.

I Can't See What You're Saying, by E. Browning, is also a personal saga of a boy and his family and their search for answers. This child was diagnosed as hard of hearing and aphasic, but so little was known about his disorder that his schooling was a hit-or-miss affair, with misunderstanding and misplacement throughout. This deficiency in language visualization in its lesser degree is the basis for many of the learning difficulties evidenced in the classroom, but in a more subtle form. It is still not fully understood or identified.

And Miles To Go . . . . by Betty Lou Kratoville, is the story of her son and their struggles from the moment the psychologist announced the boy should be institutionalized as mentally defective, through several regimes and therapies (which are discussed in *Prescriptive Teaching: Theory into Practice),* to his success in a normal fourth grade classroom setting. Problems were present, but not unsolvable, and the teachers' persistance and the programs which helped the boy can be a guide to all.

Last, we would strongly suggest the optimistic and compassionate writings of Leo Buscaglia, *Love As a Behavior Modifier,* and *Help Me! I Have an Exceptional Child,* which were two papers presented to the Texas Association for Children with Learning Disabilities in 1971. These papers were written for anyone who is truly interested in providing a learning environment where successful experiences and positive self-concept become a way of life.

GLOSSARY

acuity (visual or auditory) — sharpness or clarity of image or sound received by the viewer or listener.

ambilateral — refers to a lack of lateral dominance resulting in changing lead side (hand, foot, eye) for activities. Such persons are referred to as being ambidextrous.

associative approach — the addition of a meaningful clue to a symbol which in itself has no clue to its meaning. The purpose is to evoke recall of the symbol.

auditory closure — the process of filling in distorted or unheard portions of a word or group of words by using past experience to get at the meaning.

auditory feedback — use of self-vocalizing (talking aloud to yourself) as an attention focuser.

auditory/kinesthetic match — involves a say-and-do or a hear-and-do activity.

auditory/visual match — accurately attaching an auditory (sound or word) stimulus with its visual referent (object or symbol).

body awareness — an automatic, unconscious ability to move through space.

body concept — an intellectual knowledge of the body through consciously learning the parts and their functions; from "This is my thumb," to "My stomach is for digestion."

body image — a person's subjective experiences about his body; one's feelings about himself. For example, "I am handsome, strong, etc."

Configuration Cards — a set of cards, designed by the authors and used at Educational Guidance Services, Inc., which outline the outer shape of a word on one side, and provide on the other side in scrambled form the symbols to fill the shape. Word analysis is used to unscramble the letters.

crossed dominance — the opposite eye and hand have taken the lead. Such a person may be right handed/left eyed, or vice versa.

decoding — recognition of the meaning of the spoken word, phrase, sentence, etc. "Point to the picture of the. . . "

deficiency — a defect, imperfection, or an inadequacy

development — gradual growth or advancement through progressive changes.

developmental lag — a slower rate or a delay in development (but not a deficiency).

diagnostic testing — identification of symptoms and characteristics of a problem in order to distinguish between one disorder and another. An examination to determine the distinctive symptoms of a problem.

directional awareness — an automatic and unconscious knowledge of direction or relationship of objects to self and to each other. Refers to left and right, up and down with objects and symbols, and to geographic awareness and being able to find one's way around in new places.

discrimination (visual or auditory) — the ability to see or hear the likeness or difference between objects, sounds and/or symbols.

encoding — the recall of the name of things. Attaching the symbol to the object. "Give me the name of each of these pictures. This is a. . . "

expressive language — the meaningful use of words for the purpose of communication (spoken or written).

eye/hand coordination — smooth and coordinated movement of the hand guiding the eye (in pointing) or the eye guiding the hand (in writing). A matching of two motor systems to perform one function.

261

figure/ground perception – the ability to focus on and pull to the fore pertinent details from a background or group of details. Example: (1) seeing Mother in a crowd of people, (2) finding a word on a page of words.

fixation – the ability to accurately and automatically aim the eyes at a given point.

fusion – the ability to simultaneously integrate the data received by the two eyes into a single image.

gestalt – a greater whole gained from the parts. Example: (1) car + pet = carpet, (2) eyes + ears + nose = face.

gross motor – musculature controlling the body or large portions of it.

key card – a visually static stimulus that offers a meaningful clue to aid part-to-whole perception and recall.

Kina-Bingo – a variation of the game Bingo devised by the authors that requires a kinesthetic action in playing the game of Bingo.

Kina-writing – a term coined by the authors for their development of a method of visual/auditory/associative tracing, used to reinforce cursive style, vocabulary meaning and recognition, and spelling.

kinesthetic – learning through movement about oneself and the environment; measures received through the muscular system.

lateral dominance – a preference for one side of the body as the lead side, while the opposite side acts as a supportive one.

laterality – internal awareness of the two-sidedness of the body and its difference; used in movement, especially balance.

learning disability – a term referring to a child with average or above average intellectual potential, having no functional disorder, and no primary emotional disturbance, yet who is not learning to his potential.

learning mode – manner, style or method by which a person gains knowledge about his environment; a pattern of strengths and weaknesses.

left/right differentiation – involves messages within the body which give one an awareness of the left and right sides as separate units. This body sense is later translated to an awareness of the left/right position of objects in relation to oneself, and then in relation to each other.

linear – consisting of or pertaining to lines.

manipulative material – three-dimensional materials that can be handled and moved about. Used in learning form, size, sequencing, spatial relationships, and in intensifying data to pull a figure from its background.

midline – imaginary line from the tip of the head to the feet which separates the body into symmetrical halves. Movement across the center line of the body is important in the translation of position in space and directionality (away from and to the body changes as one moves eyes, hand, etc. across the midline).

motor development – learning to use and control the muscles which move through a pattern of overinvolvement and extraneous movement toward precision performance.

part-to-whole perception – the ability to place details (pieces) in correct relationships to each other so that a meaningful total is obtained.

perceptual constancy (visual or auditory) – recognition of an image or sound as being the same when seen or heard again, either in the same circumstances, position, etc., or in different surroundings at a different time.

perceptually impaired – unable to make adequate meaning from presented stimuli.

phonetics – referring to the symbolization of sounds by written characters.

pictograms – use of pictures in place of words to communicate information.

position in space – the perception of objects in relation to oneself and in relation to each other.

projective space — perception or concept of the spatial environment.

receptive language — the ability to take in meaningfully what is communicated in words; the ability to understand language (spoken or written).

reversal — to turn in the opposite direction; may be a horizontal or vertical reversal.

rote learner — one who memorizes or repeats information in a mechanical way without attention to basic principles, concepts, rules, or meaning.

sequential awareness (visual or auditory) — the perception of time and space order of experiences, objects or symbols.

small motor (fine motor) — musculature controlling fine motor movements as in fingers and eyes.

sound/symbol association — recognizing a sound unit and its symbol referent; these must be closely and meaningfully associated with each other for recall. In spelling, the association is made from sound to symbol, and in reading, from symbol to sound.

space/time concept — an awareness of the relationship of a visual or movement experience to the length of time it takes to produce it.

spatial relations — the ability to perceive not only the relationship of objects to oneself and to each other, but to judge distance between and amount of space consumed by each.

static visual referent — a visual presentation which remains present for viewing while working; a nonmoving object or symbol.

tactile — relating to the sense of touch. The receptors under the skin send messages to the brain about the properties of what they contact.

template — a three-dimensional cut-out of a form which can be traced around. Both the insert cut from the material and the empty space left by the cut-out section can be used to provide kinesthetic and tactile learning experiences.

three-dimensional — having the properties of height, width, and thickness. With these properties objects are easiest to see and can be handled and manipulated.

time awareness — unconscious knowledge of the passage of time.

topological space — real space; awareness of the physical environment around one and of the things in it.

tracking (visual) — the ability to follow a moving object with the eyes or to move the eyes across a line of print.

transposition — to change the position or order of two or more items or symbols with each other.

two-dimensional — having the properties of height and width, thus not manipulative and can be seen by the eyes alone. Pictures are in two dimensions and are usually representations of a three-dimensional counterpart.

visual function — the use or performance of the eyes in gathering information about the environment.

visualization — the ability to form a mental image from previously experienced stimuli.

visual/motor coordination — see eye/hand coordination.

visual skills — the effective or proficient use of the eyes in gathering information about the environment.

word analysis — the breaking down of words into their parts in order to identify the word; the phonetic approach (as opposed to sight recognition) to decoding a word.

BIBLIOGRAPHY

Abernethy, K. et al.: *Jumping Up and Down*. San Rafael, Acad Ther, 1970.

Abraham, E. M., and Pezet, A. W.: *Body, Mind and Sugar*. New York, HR & W, 1951.

Banas, N., and Willis, I. H.: Perceptual games. *Open Court Kindergarten Program*. LaSalle, Open Court, 1970.

Banas, N., and Wills, I. H.: *Success Begins With Understanding*. San Rafael, Acad Ther, 1972.

Banas, N., and Yelen, B.: *Puzzle Power*. Atlanta, Humanics, 1975.

Barr, D. F.: *Auditory Perceptual Disorders*. Springfield, Thomas. 1972.

Browning, E.: *I Can't See What You're Saying*. New York, Coward, 1972.

Buscaglia, L.: *Help Me! I Have an Exceptional Child*. Paper presented to the Texas Association for Children with Learning Disabilities, Austin, Texas, 1970.

Buscaglia, L.: *Love as a Behavior Modifier*. Paper presented to the Texas Association for Children with Learning Disabilities, Austin, Texas, 1970.

Clarke, L.: *Can't Read, Can't Write, Can't Takl Too Good Either*. In Boulanger, G. (Ed.): *How to Recognize and Overcome Dyslexia in Your Child*. New York, Walker, 1973.

Conwell, J.: *The Role of Drug Therapy*. Texas Association for Children with Learning Disabilities, Beaumont, Texas, 1970.

Cratty, B. J.: *Movement and Spatial Awareness in Blind Children and Youth*. Springfield, Thomas, 1971.

Crosby, P.: *Stars*. Champaign, Garrard, 1960.

Delacato, C. H.: *A New Start for the Child with Reading Problems*. New York, McKay, 1970.

Delacato, C. H.: *The Diagnosis and Treatment of Speech and Reading Problems*. Springfield, Thomas, 1963.

Frostig, M., and Horne, D.: *Frostig Program for the Development of Visual Perception*. Chicago, Follett, 1964.

Frostig, M., and Maslow, P.: *Movement Education Theory and Practice*. Chicago, Follett, 1970.

Furth, H. G., and Wachs, H.: *Thinking Goes to School: Piaget's Theory in Practice*. New York, Oxford U Pr, 1974.

Ginsburg, H., and Opper, S. (Eds.): *Piaget's Theory of Intellectual Development: An Introduction*. Englewood Cliffs, P-H, 1969.

Gordon, S. and Golub, R. S.: *Recreation and Socialization for the Brain Injured Child*. East Orange, New Jersey Assoc. for Brain Injured Children, 1966.

Hackett, L. C., and Jenson, R. G.: *A Guide to Movement Exploration*. Palo Alto, Peek, 1966.

Kephart, N. C.: *Slow Learner in the Classroom*, rev. Columbus, Merrill, 1971.

Kirshner, A. J.: *Training That Makes Sense*. San Rafael, Acad Ther, 1972.

Kratoville, B. L.: *And Miles to Go* . . . San Rafael, Acad Ther, 1971.

Rowen, B.: *Learning through Movement*. New York, Tchrs Coll, 1963.

Scott, Foresman & Company: *Seeing Through Arithmetic*. Glenview, author, 1964.

Wunderlich, R. C.: *Allergy, Brains, and Children Coping*. St. Petersburg, Johnny Reads, 1973.

INDEX